I0100796

HOMICIDE

HOMICIDE

A Bibliography

Compiled by Ernest Abel

Bibliographies and Indexes in Sociology, Number 11

GREENWOOD PRESS
New York • Westport, Connecticut • London

LIBRARY OF CONGRESS CATALOGING-IN-PUBLICATION DATA

Abel, Ernest L., 1943-
Homicide : a bibliography.

(Bibliographies and indexes in sociology,
ISSN 0742-6895 ; no. 11)
Includes index.
1. Homicide—Bibliography. I. Title. II. Series.
Z5703.4.M87A24 1987 [HV6515] 016.3641'523 87-7553
ISBN 0-313-25901-1 (lib. bdg. : alk. paper)

Library of Congress Catalog Card Number: 87-7553
ISBN: 0-313-25901-1
ISSN: 0742-6895

First published in 1987

Greenwood Press, Inc.
88 Post Road West, Westport, Connecticut 06881

Printed in the United States of America

The paper used in this book complies with the Permanent Paper Standard issued by the National Information Standards Organization (Z39.48-1984).

10 9 8 7 6 5 4 3 2 1

CONTENTS

PREFACE

This bibliography contains references to material in the field of homicide. As such, it includes entries published prior to 1985 that deal with various aspects of homicide including statistics, demographics, theories,legal aspects, etc. This information is taken from the scientific literature rather than the popular press.

Although comprehensive, this bibliography is by no means exhaustive. Entries were collected from many sources. Most were taken from my personal collectioin of materials and from the reference lists included in these publications.

Entries are arranged alphabetically by author. Items are numbered consecutively and are referred to by number in the Subject Index. The Subject Index serves as a further guide to the literature.

INTRODUCTION

Homicide is among the ten leading causes of death in the United States for people 35 to 54 years of age. For men and women 15 to 34, it is among the four leading causes of death. Homicide is also one of the five leading causes of death in early childhood in the United States, which has the second highest childhood homicide rate in the world.

DEFINITION

Although loss of life is implicit in the definition of homicide, there are situations in which loss of life is not considered a crime, e.g., capital punishment in which a convicted offender is executed, the slaying of enemy soldiers, shooting an escaping criminal, etc.

Criminal homicide is the killing of someone without any legal justification. In criminal law two types of homicide are recognized. First degree homicide is the intentional and premeditated killing of someone. A killing that occurs in association with another felony crime such as robbery, whether intentional or not, is also considered first degree homicide. Second degree homicide is the intentional but not premeditated killing of someone.

Although deaths associated with the purchase of certain products are generally treated in the terms of civil rather than criminal offenses, there are recent trends to indicate that when an employer or manufacturer knowingly sells defective materials, or does not remove known hazards from the work place, the officers of those corporations may be charged with the crime of corporate homicide.

Closely related to homicide is manslaughter. Involuntary manslaughter is also known as nonnegligent manslaughter and refers to the killing of someone in the context of mitigating circumstances such as the heat of passion or provocation. Involuntary or negligent manslaughter refers to the killing of someone unintentionally while behaving in a reckless manner. Another related crime, aggravated assault, differs from homicide or manslaughter only in that the victim does not die.

INCIDENCE

In the United States statistics related to homicide are collected and published annually by the Federal Bureau of Investigation in its Uniform Crime Reports. According to these statistics, about 10 out of every 100,000 Americans are murdered each year in the United States. Compared to other industrialized countries, the homicide rate in the United States is one of the highest in the world.

DEMOGRAPHIC PATTERNS

While white victims outnumber black victims in terms of numbers of homicide victims, when expressed in terms of population, the rate of violent death among black males is about twice that for white victims. Homicide is also usually an intraracial rather than interacial occurrence. On a percentage basis very few whites kill blacks and very few blacks kill whites.

Men are also much more likely to be the offender and victims of homicide than women. Although men make up about 50% of the American adult population, about 75% of all homicide victims are men. Nearly all female victims of homicide are killed by men. When women are homicide offenders, nearly all of their victims are men. Women rarely kill other women.

While there is much less data concerning the social class of either the offender or victim of criminal homicide, in general homicide usually involves people in the lower socioeconomic classes.

The age group with the highest proportion of offenders and victims is 35 to 44 years of age followed by those 15 to 24 years of age. The homicide rate among children less than four years of age in the United States is among the highest in the world. In terms of rate per population, the homicide rate among black children in certain areas of the country is considerably higher than the national rate for adults, and is even higher than the 13.6 per 100,000 rate in Northern Ireland, which has the highest overall homicide rate for any developed country in the world.

Geographically, the southern United States has the highest homicide rate in the country. The homicide rate is also considerably higher in large, compared to small cities, and is much higher in cities compared to rural areas. Within urban areas, homicides tend to occur more often in districts characterized by high rates of unemployment and percentage of families living below the poverty level.

Most homicides occur in personal residences, either in the kitchen or the bedroom. The next most common place for homicide to occur is in the street.

In most homicides the offender and victim know one another and often have some personal relationships. This may be either a family relationship, or one involving friends, neighbors or acquaintances.

Most homicides take place on Saturdays and Sundays; the fewest homicides occur on Mondays and Tuesdays.

Several studies have noted a higher occurrence of homicides during the summer compared to winter but differences have been relatively small and results from other studies are contradictory.

In many cases, the offender or victim also have previous records of arrests for assault or other criminal activity. A final consideration worth noting in the context of homicide is that about 50% of all homicides the victims had been drinking shortly before their deaths. In contrast, prior use of drugs occurs much less frequently in the context of homicide. The percentage of homicide victims drinking prior to death is highest for those 25 to 34 years of age whereas for traffic accidents, the highest percentage of victims drinking prior to death is 15-24.

By far the greatest number of homicides involves guns. About two-thirds of all homicides in the United States are gun related and the U.S., homicide rate involving guns is the highest in the world. A distant second are Australia, Canada and Italy. The next most commonly used weapon in homicide is knives. Interestingly, alcohol is more commonly found in connection with homicide due to stabbings than those involving guns.

EXPLANATIONS

Psychiatric. Early attempts at explaining homicide focussed primarily on the offender and sought to explain his actions in psychiatric terms. These studies regarded homicide offenders as people with a personality disorder. Very often the offender was regarded as someone irrational or insane. Supporting this notion of irrational behavior were the facts that most offenders kill people they know rather than strangers and people with whom they have a personal relationship. Homicide is also a spontaneous rather than a premeditated act, without any planning and without any attempt to hide the offense or to prevent arrest. There is usually no motive other than a quarrel.

Since homicide seems so irrational, it was assumed that the offender was in an irrational state when he committed the crime. This irrational state was generally traced to some long-standing personality disorder. For the psychoanalyst, homicide is the result of poor impulse control stemming from a weak ego or superego that should inhibit aggressive behavior. Failure to develop these ego or superego restraints is sometimes traced to family settings in which the offender received less than adequate nurturing as a child. As a result he/she failed to develop mechanisms for internalizing aggression in socially acceptable ways.

Victim - Precipitated Homicide. Another explanation focuses on victim precipitation. In this context, it is the victim who first threatens the offender with some weapon. In an attempt to defend himself the offender kills the victim. Studies of victim precipitated homicide point to regularities in demographic patterns such as race, sex and age as support for the notion that many homicides are precipitated by common factors.

Subculture of Violence. A third theme in homicide studies is sociological. This approach argues that homicide is not an irrational behavior but one that is both rational and typical of the social milieu in which the offender lives and develops. This approach emphasizes a subculture of violence and regards or examines behavior in the context of this subculture rather than the total culture. Behavior that might be considered unreasonable or inappropriate to the culture as a whole might be very appropriate to a section of the culture. If the subculture expects its members to react with violence to any insult or threat, imagined or real, assault becomes the norm rather than the irrational response. If such an assault results in death this would be considered a justifiable homicide by the members of the subculture. Members of the subculture who do not react in the appropriate way (i.e. react violently), are ostracized and ridiculed into conformity.

Frustration - aggression. This hypothesis argues that economic inequality results in frustration and frustration results in aggression. Frustration occurs in societies that emphasize and respect economic achievement, but restrict opportunities for achieving such economic success. This occurs most often in minority groups. Since members of these groups are frustrated in their efforts to achieve their goals, they react to this frustration with violent behavior.

Gamesmanship. A fifth view of homicide looks at it in terms of gamesmanship taken to the extreme. In the game, the offender and victim each try to maintain their own integrity or identity while belittling the integrity or identity of the other. Contestants typically start off by challenging the sincerity of the other as friend or spouse. The confrontation results in some accusation and threat of force. The intent is to make the other person back down. The threat of violence has the effect of escalating the confrontation from a verbal to a physical settlement. If either contestant backs down he loses face; if he retaliates, a physical confrontation becomes inevitable. The more aggressive the victim or offender, the more likely the confrontation will result in homicide. Also, if either of the participants have a weapon, especially a gun, the confrontation is one likely to result in a homicide.

DETERRENCE

Homicide is considered one of the most serious of crimes and carries with it very punitive measures including death. Capital punishment is considered by many as a deterrent to homicide. This is based on the belief that people act rationally and will not engage in activities which could result in loss of their own lives. However, there is little evidence to indicate that capital punishment does act as a deterrent to homicide. Studies that have compared homicide rates between states with capital punishment and those that do not have capital punishment, and studies comparing homicide statistics within states prior to enactment of capital punishment laws with homicide rates following enactment of capital punishment, have rarely found significant differences due to capital punishment. Another argument against capital punishment is that homicide is an irrational rather than a rational form of behavior. As such, the offender is unlikely to consider the consequences of his actions. If the possibility of capital punishment is not even a consideration in the offender's mind, then capital punishment cannot act as a deterrent. Opponents of capital punishment also contend that capital punishment by its very nature is no different than the act being punished. If homicide is morally objectionable for the individual, opponents of capital punishment argue that it is also morally objectionable for the state.

HOMICIDE

BIBLIOGRAPHY

A

1. Abel, E., Strasburger, L. and Zeidenberg, P. Seasonal, monthly, and day-of-week trends in homicide as affected by alcohol and race. Alc Clin Exp Res 1985, 9, 281-283.

2. Abel, E. & Zeidenberg, P. Age, alcohol and violent death: A postmortem study. J Stud Alc. 1985, 46, 228-231.

3. Abel, E., Zeidenberg, P. & Regan, S. Alcohol and violent death-Erie County, N.Y., 1973-1983. MMWR 1984, 33, 226-234.

4. Abrahamsen, D. Detecting the Potentially Violent Person. In: Abrahamsen, D. (ed). Our Violent Society. Funk and Wagnalls, N.Y., 1970, 209-236.

5. Abrahamsen, D. The Murdering Mind. Harper & Row, N.Y., 1975.

6. Abrahamsen, D. The dynamic connection between personality and crime and the detection of the potential criminal illustrated by different types of murder. J Crim Psychopath. 1944, 481-8.

7. Abrahamsen, D. Crime and the Human Mind. Columbia Univ Press, N.Y. 1944.

8. Adelson, L. The Pathology of Homicide: Avade Mecum for Pathologist, Prosecutor and Defense Counsel. C.C. Thomas, Springfield, Ill., 1974.

9. Agopian, M.W., Chappell, D., Geis, G. Interracial Forcible Rape in a North American City: An Analysis of Sixty-Three Cases. In: Drapkin, I. (ed). Victimology, Lexington Books, Lexington, Mass, 1974, 93-102.

10. Ahlstrom, W.M., Havighurst, R.J. The World They Live In. In: Ahlstrom, W. (ed). 400 Losers. Jossey-Bass, San Francisco, 1971, 141-153.

11. Ahronheim, J.C., Bernholc, A.S. & Clark, W.D. Age trends in autopsy rates. Striking decline in late life. JAMA. 1983, 250, 1182-6.

12. Akbar, N. Homicide among black males. Causal factors. Pub Hlth Rep. 1980, 95, 554-6.

13. Akbar, N. Causal factors. Pub Hlth Rep. 1980, 95, 554-555.

14. Akiyama, Y. Murder victimization: A statistical analysis. Law Enforce Bull. 1981, 50, 3, 8-11.

15. Alexander, G.R., Massey, R.M., Gibbs, T. & Altekruse, J.M. Firearm-related fatalities: an epidemiologic assessment of violent death. Am J Pub Hlth. 1985, 75, 165-8.

16. Alha, A.R., Parviainen, A.R. & Tamminen, V.K. Forensic chemical examinations in Finland, 1979--trends in fatal poisoning. J Forens Sci. 1981, 26, 758-65.

17. Allen, H.D. & Bankston, W.B. Another look at the southern culture of violence hypothesis: The case of Louisiana. South Sociol Soc. 1978, 1230.

18. Allen, H.D., McSeveney, D.R. & Bankston, W.B. The influence of southern culture on race-specific homicide rates. Sociol Spect. 1981, 1, 4, 361-374.

19. Allen, N.H. Homicide followed by suicide: Los Angeles, 1970-1979. Suicide Life Threat Behav. 13, 155-65, 1983.

20. Allen, N.H. Homicide prevention and intervention. Suicide Life Threat Behav. 11, 3, 167-79, 1981.

21. Allen, N.H. Homicide: Perspectives on Prevention. Human Sciences Press, N.Y., 1980.

22. Allison, R.B. Difficulties diagnosing the multiple personality syndrome in a death penalty case. Int J Clin Exp Hypn. 1984, 32, 102-17.

23. Al-Najjar, S-Y. Suicide and Islamic law. Ment Hlth Soc. 1976, 3, 137-141.

24. Altick, R.D. Victorian Studies in Scarlet, Norton, N.Y., 1970.

25. Altman, J., Ziporyn, M. Born to Raise Hell: The Untold Story of Richard Speck. Grove Press, N.Y., 1967, 255.

26. Amatuzio, J.C. & Coe, J.I. Homicide by exploder ammunition. Am J Forens Med Pathol. 1981, 2, 111-113.

27. Anable, W.R. Homicidal threat as grief work. Psychiat Opin. 1978, 15, 43-47.

28. Andahl, R.O. The examination of saw marks. J Forensic Sci Soc. 1978, 18, 31-46.

29. Anderson, D.S. Corporate homicide: the stark realities of artificial beings and legal fictions. Pepperdine Law Rev. 1981, 367-417.

30. Anderson, P.C. Murder in medical education. JAMA 1968, 204, 21-5.

31. Anderson, W.P. & Holcomb, W.R. Accused murderers: five MMPI personality types. J Clin Psychol. 1983, 39, 761-8.

32. Anonymous. Alcohol and fatal injuries--Fulton County, Georgia, 1982. MMWR. 1983, 32, 573-6.

33. Anonymous. Automobile homicide. Utah Law Rev. 1982, 1, 139-143.

34. Anonymous. Barring slayers' acquisition of property rights in Virginia: a proposed statute. Univ Rich Law Rev. 1979, 1, 251-277.

35. Anonymous. Case law development and mental disability./Section II: case law developments. Ment Disab Law Rep. 1976, 1, 183-205.

36. Anonymous. Causing death by reckless driving. Crim Law Rev. 1984, 431-432.

37. Anonymous. Child homicide--United States. MMWR. 1982, 31, 292-4.

38. Anonymous. Children who allegedly witnessed murder--require psychiatric exam. Ment Hlth Court Digest. 1976, 19, 1.

39. Anonymous. Coroner's procedure in homicide. Br Med J. 1959, 59.

40. Anonymous. Criminal law and procedure. Utah Law Rev. 1984, 1, 130-164.

41. Anonymous. Criminal negligence held required to support conviction for automobile homicide. Utah Law Rev. 1981, 1, 190-194.

42. Anonymous. Defendant held to have known what he was doing when pleading guilty. Ment Hlth Court Digest. 1974, 17, 4.

43. Anonymous. Defining the crime of murder. J Crim Law. 1921, 12, 121-3.

44. Anonymous. Degree of drunkenness necessary to reduce a murder from first to second degree. Tenn Law Rev. 1946, 19, 486-7.

45. Anonymous. Degrees of murder and manslaughter. West Va Law Quart. 1938, 44, 194-205.

46. Anonymous. Distinction between handling of insanity and "Diminished Capacity": Ment Hlth Court Digest. 1974, 18, 4.

47. Anonymous. Doctor's opinion of sexual psycho-pathology not admissible evidence. Ment Hlth Court Digest. 1975, 18, 5.

48. Anonymous. Dr. Leonard Arthur: his trial and its implications. Br Med J, 1981, 283, 1340-1.

49. Anonymous. Drug abuse among students in the State of Minas Gerais, Brazil. Bull Narcot. 1979, 31, 49-58.

50. Anonymous. Echovirus type 30: 1980. Br Med J [Clin Res], 1981, 282, 1083-4.

51. Anonymous. Effects of L.S.D. Br Med J. 1966, 5502, 1495-1496.

52. Anonymous. Escapee in stolen car kills another car driver--State not liable. Ment Hlth Court Digest. 1972, 15, 1.

53. Anonymous. Evidence-admissibility of evidence of a homicide victim's character where the defendant pleads self-defense. Suffolk Univ Law Rev. 1979, 13, 1135-49.

54. Anonymous. Evidence--evidence of prior similar incidents is admissible to show the corpus delicti of murder. Univ Cinc Law Rev. 1974, 43, 437-43.

55. Anonymous. Evidence of uncommunicated threats in excusable homicide cases. Ark Law Rev. 1951, 5, 207-13.

56. Anonymous. Evidence--presumptions--application of the deadly weapons presumption in West Virginia. W Virg Law Rev. 1973, 75, 287.

57. Anonymous. Evidence-proof of murder without a body--sufficience of circumstantial evidence to prove the corpus delicti in a murder prosecution. Vill Law Rev. 1960, 5, 685.

58. Anonymous. Evidence--proof of particular facts--evidence that defendant may have committed similar crimes is admissible to prove corpus delicti of murder. Harv Law Rev. 1974, 87, 1074-81.

59. Anonymous. Felony murder in Georgia: a lethal anachronism? Ga State Bar J. 1973, 9, 462.

60. Anonymous. Feticide is still legal in Louisiana. Loyola Law Rev. 1980, 26, 422-30.

61. Anonymous. Fetus as a legal entity -- facing reality. San Diego Law Rev. 1971, 8, 126.

62. Anonymous. First and second degree murder and their distinguishing requirements in Idaho. Idaho Law Rev. 1965, 2, 77.

63. Anonymous. First degree murder indictment of parents--child neglected. Soc Welf Court Digest. 1971, 16, 1.

64. Anonymous. First degree murder--premeditation and deliberation. Ark Law Rev. 1949-1950, 4, 92-4.

65. Anonymous. Forensic medicine. Bull Med Leg Toxicol Med 1968, 11, 264-277.

66. Anonymous. George Armstrong Custer and the battle of the Little Bighorn: homicide or mass suicide? J Forens Sci. 1983, 3, 756-761.

67. Anonymous. Guilty and insane verdict upheld. Ment Physic Disabil Law Rep. 1984, 8, 17.

68. Anonymous. Guns: Bicentennial note. Crime Delinq. 1976, 22, 2.

69. Anonymous. Handguns and homicide. JAMA 1977, 237(15),1558-9.

70. Anonymous. Hlth promotion: Control of stress and violent behavior. Pub Hlth Rep. 1983, 167-76.

71. Anonymous. Historical development of self-defense as an excuse for homicide. Ky Law J. 1951, 39, 469-71.

72. Anonymous. Homicide Among Black Males. Highlights of the symposium sponsored by the Alcohol, Drug Abuse, and Mental Health Administration, Washington, D.C., May 13--14, 1980.

73. Anonymous. Homicide and suicide by Army sergeant after hospital release--no case. Ment Hlth Court Digest. 1976, 20, 6.

74. Anonymous. Homicide in the United States - 1950-1964 - Vital Hlth Statist. 1967, 20, 6, 33.

75. Anonymous. Homicide on the uptrend. Statist Bull Metrop Life Ins Co. 1968, 49.

76. Anonymous. "Homicide scene" exception to the fourth amendment warrant requirement: a dead issue? J Crim Law. 1980, 71, 289-99.

77. Anonymous. Homicide--United States. MMWR. 1982, 31, 600-2.

78. Anonymous. Hospital crimes and hazards--forensic aspects. Forens Sci Int. 1982, 19, 289-93.

79. Anonymous. Indiana's statutory protection for the abused child. Valparaiso Univ Law Rev. 1974, 9, 89-133.

80. Anonymous. Irresistible impulse. Br Med J. 1960, 1283-4.

81. Anonymous. Is the intentional killing of an unborn child homicide? Pacific Law J. 1971, 2, 179.

82. Anonymous. Justifiable homicide, defense of intoxicating liquor illegally possessed. Virg Law Rev. 1933, 19, 301-2.

83. Anonymous. Killing of a viable fetus is murder. Md Law Rev. 1970, 30, 137.

84. Anonymous. Leads from the MMWR. Violent deaths among persons 15 to 24 years of age--United States. JAMA. 1983, 250, 3147-8.

85. Anonymous. Legal position of euthanasia: an expert opinion. Aust Nurses J. 1984, 14, 57.

86. Anonymous. Liability and immunity issues. Ment Physic Disabil Law Rep. 1984, 8, 402-403.

87. Anonymous. Madness, responsibility and the law. Nature. 1981, 291, 367-8.

88. Anonymous. Manslaughter and causing death by reckless driving. J Crim Law. 1983, 1, 40-43.

89. Anonymous. Manslaughter and the adequacy of provocation: the reasonableness of the reasonable man. Univ Penn Law Rev. 1958, 106,1021.

90. Anonymous. Manslaughter by motor cars. Fortnightly Law J. 1942, 12, 118-21.

91. Anonymous. Manslaughter by neglect. Br Med J. 1977, 1, 722-3.

92. Anonymous. Manslaughter charges against doctors. Br Med J. 1975, 2, 287-8.

93. Anonymous. Manslaughter provocation - criminal and forceful relations and spouse. Univ Pitts Law Rev. 1950, 11, 709-11.

94. Anonymous. Massacre at Lebach arms depot in Federal Germany. Int Crim Pol Rev. 1974, 28, 154-161.

95. Anonymous. Mentally disabled man convicted of murder. Ment Physic Disabil Law Rep. 1984.

96. Anonymous. M'naughten rule applied in California. Ment Physic Disabil Law Report. 1984, 8, 518-519.

97. Anonymous. M`Naughten test upheld--Murder conviction reversed. Ment Hlth Court Digest. 1974, 18, 5.

98. Anonymous. Murder and the Murderer. Nelson-Hall, Chicago, 1975.

99. Anonymous. Murder conviction upheld despite lack of direct evidence of corpus delicti. Colum Law Rev. 1961, 61, 740.

100. Anonymous. Murder in first degree, evidence, confessions. St. John's Law Rev. 1929, 3, 284-5.

101. Anonymous. Murder 1957 to 1968. Mod Law Rev. 1970, 33, 302.

102. Anonymous. Murder scene warrantless searches: a proposal. Ariz Law Rev. 1979, 21, 776-93.

103. Anonymous. Murderers. Med J Aust. 1979, 1, 283-4.

104. Anonymous. Murderers. Med J Aust. 1979, 1, 283-4.

105. Anonymous. Murderers, madmen, and mores. Stanford Law Rev. 1968, 1, 134-6.

106. Anonymous. Nature of precipitating crime found key to homicide analysis. Crim Just Newsl. 1985, 17, 3.

107. Anonymous. New crime of genocide. Br Med J. 1969, 3, 422, 16.

108. Anonymous. N.Y., Montana and Alaska Determine Diminished Capacity. Ment Disabil Law Rep. 1980, 4, 229-230.

109. Anonymous. No right to counsel during psychiatric examination after insanity plea in Illinois. Ment Disabil Law Rep. 1979, 3, 166.

110. Anonymous. No right to incompetency hearing - after guilt. Ment Hlth Court Digest. 1973, 16, 4.

111. Anonymous. Non-consensual destruction of the fetus - abortion or homicide? UCLA-Alaska Law Rev. 1971, 1, 80.

112. Anonymous. Non-consensual killing of an unborn infant: a criminal act? Buffalo Law Rev. 1971, 20, 535.

113. Anonymous. Non-intervention in children with major handicaps. Legal and ethical issues. Aust Paediatr J. 1983, 19, 217-22.

114. Anonymous. Nursing home administrator convicted of resident abuse. Ment Physic Disabil Law Rep. 1984, 8, 474.

115. Anonymous. Physician murderers and criminals. Forens Sci Int. 1982, 20, 101-6.

116. Anonymous. Physicians negligent in discharging mental patient who murdered family. J Miss State Med Assoc., 1984, 25, 276, 284.

117. Anonymous. Prevention of homicide. Br Med J. 1979, 1, 774.

118. Anonymous. Proof of the corpus deliciti by circumstantial evidence where the body is never found. W Virg Law Rev. 1961, 63, 156.

119. Anonymous. Proposed Wisconsin rules of evidence: 905.04., physician, psychologist-patient privilege. Marquette Law Rev. 1973, 56, 248-251.

120. Anonymous. Proving live birth in infanticide. Wyo Law J. 1963, 17, 237.

121. Anonymous. Psychiatry and homicide. Br Med J. 1976, 1, 1300.

122. Anonymous. Psychotherapist-patient privilege discussed. Ment Physic Disabil Law Rep. 1984, 8, 41-42.

123. Anonymous. Reckless driving causing death. J Crim Law. 1981, 3, 155-156.

124. Anonymous. Recklessness in manslaughter and reckless driving. J Crim Law. 1983, 4, 229-232.

125. Anonymous. Reg. v. Dr. Leonard Arthur. Med J Aust. 1982, 2, 558-60.

126. Anonymous. Somnambulistic homicide. Br Med J. 1961, 5239, 1616.

127. Anonymous. Subjective or objective test of presumptions in murder cases. Law Quart Rev. 1961, 77, 1.

128. Anonymous. Suicide statistics: The problem of comparability. WHO Chronicle. 1975, 29, 188-192.

129. Anonymous. Survey of felony murder. Temp Law Quart. 1955, 28, 453-66.

130. Anonymous. Sutcliffe and after. Lancet. 1981, 1, 1241-2.

131. Anonymous. The burden of responsibility. JAMA. 1967, 199, 112.

132. Anonymous. The Guyana tragedy--an international forensic problem. Forens Sci Int. 1979, 13, 167-72.

133. Anonymous. The murderer and his victim's insurance money. Sol J. 1930, 74, 32.

134. Anonymous. The Scott-Elliott murders. Med Leg J. 1982, 50, 140-58.

135. Anonymous. Trouble in the family: A case of patricide. Pract Psychol Physic. 1975, 2, 40-42.

136. Anonymous. Unusual blood evidence in a homicide a century ago. Am J Forens Med Pathol. 1982, 3, 231-9.

137. Anonymous. Violent deaths among persons 15-24 years of age--United States, 1970-1978. MMWR. 1983, 32, 453-7.

138. Anonymous. Vital and Health Statistics. Homicide in the United States, 1950-1964. Nat Cent Hlth Stat. Washington, DC, 1967.

139. Anonymous. Voluntary drunkenness as a defense to murder. Virg Law Rev. 1938, 24, 926-7.

140. Anonymous. Warrantless murder scene searches in the aftermath of Mincey v. Arizona. Wash Univ Law Quart. 1980, 58, 367-408.

141. Anonymous. Wrongful death. Am Fam Physic. 1982, 26, 113.

142. Anthi, P.R. The primal scene in Sandemose's murder mysteries: creativity in writing and in psychoanalytic treatment. Scand Psychoanal Rev. 1982, 5, 91-104.

143. Anthony, H.S. The association of violence and depression in a sample of young offenders. Br J Criminol. 1968, 4, 346-365.

144. Anthony, J.E. & Koupernik, C. The Child in His Family: The Impact of Disease and Death. John Wiley & Son, Inc., N.Y., 1973.

145. Antunes, G., Hunt, A.L. The impact of certainty and severity of punishment on levels of crime in American states: An extended analysis. J Crim Law Criminol. 1973 64, 486-493.

146. Appelbaum, P.S. Law & Psychiatry. Death, the expert witness, and the dangers of going barefoot. Hosp Commun Psychiat. 1983, 34, 1003-4.

147. Aprahamian, C., Thompson, B.M., Towne, J.B., Darin, J.C. The effect of a paramedic system on mortality of major open intra-abdominal vascular trauma. J Trauma. 1983, 23, 687-90.

148. Arado, C.C. Homicides committed in drunken brawls. J Crim Law. 1932, 23, 473-8.

149. Arado, C.C. Murder by abandoned colored youths. J Crim Law. 1932, 23, 469-73.

150. Arboleda-Florez, J. Amok. Bull Am Acad Psychiat Law. 1979, 7, 286-95.

151. Arboleda, F.J. Infanticide: Some medicolegal considerations. Can Psychiat Assoc J. 1975, 20, 55-60.

152. Arboleda, F.J. Neonaticide. Can Psychiat Assoc J. 1976, 21, 31-34.

153. Arboleda-Florez, J. Post-homicide psychotic reaction. Int J Offend Ther Comp Criminol. 25:47-52, 1981.

154. Arboleda-Florez, J. Infanticide: Some medicolegal considerations. Can Psychiat Assoc J. 1975, 20, 55-60.

155. Arbuthnot, J. Attributions of responsibility by simulated jurors: stage of moral reasoning and guilt by association. Psychol Rep. 1983, 52, 287-98.

156. Archer, D., Gartner, R. & Beittel, M. Homicide and the death penalty: A cross-national test of a deterrence hypothesis. J Crim Law Criminol. 1983, 74, 991-1013.

157. Archer, D., Gartner, R. Violent acts and violent times: a comparative approach to postwar homicide rates. Am Sociol Rev.. 41:937-963, 1976.

158. Archer, D., Gartner, R., Akert, R. & Lockwood, T. Cities and homicide: A new look at an old paradox. Comparat Stud Sociol. 1978, 1, 73-95.

159. Aremu, L.O. Criminal responsibility for homicide in Nigeria and supernatural beliefs. Int Comp Law Quart. 1980, 1, 112-131.

160. Arieti, S. & Schrieber, F.R. Multiple murders of a schizophrenic patient: a psychodynamic interpretation. J Am Acad Psychoanal. 1981, 9, 501-24.

161. Arena, C. Helping children deal with the death of a classmate: A crisis intervention model. Elem School Guid Counsel. 1984, 19, 107-15.

162. Argeriou, M. Daily alcohol consumption patterns in Boston: Some findings and a partial test of the Tuesday hypothesis. J Stud Alc 1974, 36, 1578-1583.

163. Armstrong, R.W. & Matsuoka, N.S. Epidemiologic patterns of homicides in the city & county of Honolulu, 1977-1983. Hawaii Med J. 1984, 43, 230-6.

164. Arnold, Law, Fleming, R. & Bell, V. The man who became angry once: a study of overcontrolled hostility. Can J Psychiat. 1979, 24, 762-6.

165. Artzt, E. Is There Something about America... In: Hartogs, R. (ed). Violence: Causes and Solutions. Dell, N.Y., 1970.

166. Asberg, M., Bertilsson, L. & Martensson, B. CSF monoamine metabolites, depression, and suicide. Adv Biochem Psychopharmacol. 1984, 39, 87-97.

167. Ashall, P.A. Manslaughter - the impact of Caldwell? Crim Law Rev. 1984, 467-476.

168. Ashman, A. Viable fetus is a person in Massachusetts. Am Bar Assoc J. 1984, 120.

169. Ashworth, A.J. Self-induced provocation and the homicide act. Crim Law Rev. 1973, 1973, 483-92.

170. Ashworth, A.J. Short note on the English murder rate. Crim Law Rev. 1969, 1969-645.

171. Asnaes, S. & Paaske, F. Uncertainty of determining mode of death in medicolegal material without autopsy--a systematic autopsy study. Forens Sci Int. 1980, 15, 3-17.

172. Asuni, T. Homicide in western Nigeria. Br J Psychiat. 1973, 115, 1105-1113.

173. Asuni, T. Attempted suicide in western Nigeria. Cent Afr J Med. 1967, 13, 289.

174. Athens, L.H. A symbolic interactionist's approach to violent criminal acts. Diss Abs Intern. 1976, 37, 627-628.

175. Atkinson, G. Killing and letting die: hidden value assumptions. Soc Sci Med. 1983, 17, 1915-25.

176. Atkinson, G.M. Ambiguities in 'killing'and 'letting die'. J Med Philos. 1983, 8, 159-68.

177. Averill, J.R. Anger. Nebr Symp Motiv. 1978, 26, 1-80.

178. Avison, N.H. Victims of Homicide. Intern J Criminol Penol. 1974, 2, 225-237.

B

179. Bailey, W.C. Use of the death penalty v. outrage at murder: some additional evidence and considerations. J Crime Delinq. 1976, 22, 31-39.

180. Bailey, W.C. Poverty, inequality, and city homicide rates; Some not so unexpected findings. Criminol. 1984, 22, 531-550.

181. Bailey, W.C. Capital punishment and lethal assaults against police. Criminol. 1982, 19, 608-625.

182. Bailey, W.C. A multivariate cross-sectional analysis of the deterrent effect of the death penalty. Sociol Social Res. 1980, 64, 183-207.

183. Bailey, W.C. & Smith R.W. Punishment: Its severity and certainty. J Crim Law Criminol Pol Sci. 1972, 63, 530-539.

184. Bailey, W.C. Disaggregation in deterrence and death penalty research: The case of murder in Chicago. J Crim Law Criminol. 1983, 74, 827-859.

185. Bailey, W.C. Deterrent effect of the death penalty: An extended time series analysis. J Death Dying. 1979, 10, 235-259.

186. Bailey, W.C. Homicide and a Regional Culture of Violence: Some Further Evidence. In: M. Riedel & T.P. Thornberry (eds). Crime and Delinquency: Dimensions of Deviance, Praeger, N.Y., 1974.

187. Baker, J.L. Indians, alcohol, and homicide. J Soc Ther. 1959, 5, 270-275.

188. Baker, J.S. Criminal law: Developments in the law, 1981-1982: A symposium. La Law Rev. 1982, 2, 361-374.

189. Baker, S.P. Without guns, do people kill people? Am J Public Hlth. 1985, 75, 587-8.

190. Baker, S.P. Tatoos, alcohol, and violent death. J Forens Sci. 1971, 16, 219-25.

191. Bakwin, H. Homicidal deaths in infant and children. J Pediat. 1960, 57, 568-70.

192. Baldock, D.V. Attempted murder by calor gas. J Forens Sci Soc. 1970, 10, 175-8.

193. Baldwin, J.A. Deaths from non-accidental injury in children. Br Med J. 1980, 280, 1533.

194. Balthazar, M.L. & Cook, R.J. An analysis of the factors related to the rate of violent crimes committed by incarcerated female delinquents. Special issue: Gender issues, sex offenses, and criminal justice: Current trends. J Offend Counsel Service Rehabil. 1984, 9, 103-118.

195. Banay, R.S. A study of twenty-two men convicted of murder in the first degree. J Crim Law Criminol. 1943, 34, 106-111.

196. Banks, J. & Vatz, D. Sinusoidal pattern analysis in criminal incidence. Criminol. 1976, 14, 2, 251-258.

197. Bankston, W.B. & Allen, D. Rural social areas and patterns of homicide: An analysis of lethal violence in Louisiana. Rural Sociol. 1980, 45, 223-237.

198. Barber, R.N. & Wilson, P.R. Deterrent aspect of capital punishment and its effect on conviction rates: The Queensland experience. Austral NZ J Criminol. 1968, 1, 100-108.

199. Bard, M. Assaultiveness and alcohol use in family disputes: Police perceptions. Criminol. 1974, 3, 281-292.

200. Barker, E.T. & Mason, M.H. The insane criminal as therapist. Can J Correct. 1968. 10, 553-561.

201. Barnard, G.W., Vera, H., Vera, M.I. & Newman, G. Till death do us part: a study of spouse murder. Bull Am Acad Psychiat Law. 1982, 10, 271-80.

202. Barnes, F.C. A death from an air gun. J Forens Sci. 1976, 21, 653-8.

203. Barnes, F.C. and Helson, R.A. An empirical study of gunpowder residue patterns. J Forens Sci. 1974, 19, 448-462.

204. Barnett, A. Learning to live with homicide: a research note. J Crim Just. 1982, 1, 69-72.

205. Barnett, A., Essenfeld, E. and Kleitman, D.J. Urban homicide: some recent developments. J Crim Just. 1980, 8, 379-385.

206. Barnett, A. Crime and capital punishment: Some recent studies. J Crim Just. 1978, 6, 291-303.

207. Barnett, A., Kleitman, D.J. and Larson, R.C. On urban homicide: a statistical analysis. J Crim Just. 1975, 3, 85-110.

208. Barnett, A. & Kleitman, D.J. Urban violence and risk to the individual. J Res Crime Delinq. 1973, 10, 111-116.

209. Barnett, G.V. & Franke, R.H. "Psychogenic" death: A reappraisal. Science. 1970, 167, 304-306.

210. Barney, C.E. Malice, presumption of malice from use of deadly weapon. Neb Law B. 1938, 17, 231-5.

211. Barron, J. Confidentiality and the duty to warn. Ohio Nurses Rev. 1983, 58, 12-3.

212. Bartholomew, A.A., Milte, K.L. & Galbally, F. Epileptic homicide. Br J Psychiat. 1978, 133, 564-5.

213. Bartholomew, A.A. Homosexual necrophilia. Med Sci Law. 1978, 18, 29-35.

214. Barzun, J. Doctors criminal and criminous. N Engl J Med. 1971, 284, 710-3.

215. Bascue, L.O. & Epstein, L. Suicide attitudes and experiences of hospitalized alcoholics. Psychol Rep. 1980, 47, 1233-1234.

216. Bass, J.L, Gallagher, S.S. & Mehta, K.A. Injuries to adolescents and young adults. Pediatr Clin North Am. 1985, 32, 31-9.

217. Bates, G.M., Jr. Homicidal acts of war. Am J Psychiat. 1972, 129, 766.

218. Bates, M.L.D. Murder convictions for homicides committed in the course of driving while intoxicated. Cumberland Law Rev. 1977, 8, 477-494.

219. Bauman, W.A. & Yalow, R.S. Insulin as a lethal weapon. J Forens Sci. 1981, 26, 594-8.

220. Bautista, A.L. Liability of a stranger who participates in the crime of parricide. Phil Law J. 1940, 19, 326-8.

221. Baxley, R.C. Voluntary intoxication from phencyclidine. Will it raise a reasonable doubt of the mental capacity of a person charged with a crime requiring specific intent or mental state? J Psychedel Drugs. 1980, 12, 331-5.

222. Baxter, S.J. & Rees, B. The immunological identification of foetal haemoglobin in bloodstains in infanticide and associated crimes. Med Sci Law. 1974, 14, 163-167.

223. Bayaert, F.H. The Dutch situation and some problems. Int J Law Psychiat. 1980, 3, 173-8.

224. Bean, F.D., Cushing, R.G. Criminal homicide, punishment and deterrence: Methodological and substantive reconsiderations. Soc Sci Quart. 52, 277-289, 1972.

225. Beasley, R.W. & Atunes, G. The etiology of urban crime: An ecological analysis. Criminol. 1974, 11, 4, 439-461.

226. Beckett, J.S. Speaking from the grave--a homicide victim's antecedent accusatory statements about the defendant. Ill Bar J. 1982, 4, 250-256.

227. Bedau, H.A. Rough justice: the limits of novel defenses. Hastings Cent Rep. 1978, 8, 8-11.

228. Beddoe, H.L. Hit-run murders: examination of the body. J Crim Law. 1958, 49, 280.

229. Bednarczyk, L.R. & Matusiak, W. Case report: an arsenic murder. J Anal Toxicol. 1982, 6, 260-1.

230. Behemer, G.K. Deadly motherhood: Infanticide and medical opinion in Med-Victorian England. J Hist Med Allied Sci. 1979, 34, 403-437.

231. Bell, C.C. Interface between psychiatry and the law on the issue of murder. J Nat Med Assoc. 1980, 72, 1093-7.

232. Bell, D. Jack the Ripper-The final solution? Criminologist. 1974, 9, 40.

233. Belleau, T. & Arsenian, J. Homicide and hospitalization: A case report. Psychiatry. 1967, 30, 1, 73-78.

234. Bellen, E.J. American defence legal systems in Germany. Med Sci Law. 1981, 21, 10-5.

235. Bender, Law A psychiatrist looks at deviancy as a factor in juvenile delinquency. Fed Probat. 1968-9, 32, 35-42.

236. Bender, Law and Curran, F.J. Children and adolescents who kill. J Crim Psychopath. 1940, 1, 297-322.

237. Bender. Psychiatric mechanisms in child murderers. J Nerv Ment Dis 1934, 80, 32-47.

238. Bendheim, O.L. The psychiatric autopsy: its legal application. Bull Am Acad Psychiat Law. 1979, 7, 400-10.

239. Benenson, M.K. A controlled look at gun controls. N.Y. Law Forum. 1968, 14, 718-748.

240. Benezech, M., Yesavage, J.A., Addad, M., Bourgeois, M. & Mills, M. Homicide by psychotics in France: a five-year study. J Clin Psychiat. 1984, 45, 85-6.

241. Benezech, M., Bourgeois, M. Boukhabza, D. & Yesavage, J.A. Cannibalism and vampirism in paranoid schizophrenia. J Clin Psychiat. 1981, 42, 290.

242. Bennett, L.J. Psychiatric diagnosis in the witness box: a postscript on the 'Yorkshire Ripper' trial. Bull Brit Psychol Soc. 1981, 34, 305-307.

243. Bennett, G.T. & Sullwold, A.F. Qualifying the psychiatrist as a lay witness: a reaction to the American Psychiatric Association petition in Barefoot v. Estelle. J Forens Sci. 1985, 30, 462-6.

244. Bennington, J. Having mental age of boy of nine - appropriate age for "reasonable man" under the section. Crim Law Rev 1982, 51-52.

245. Bensing, R.C. & Schroeder, O. Homicide in an Urban Community. C.C. Thomas, Springfield, Ill., 1958.

246. Bentil, J.K. Indirectly causing death of another as homicide. Solicitor's J. 1984, 29, 493-495.

247. Bentil, J.K. Homicide and elements of diminishing responsibility. Solicitor's J. 1983, 36, 590-592.

248. Bentil, J.K. Mental imbalance and diminished responsibility in homicide. Solicitor's J. 1981, 4, 54-56.

249. Bentil, J.K. Homicide and evidence and reports of psychiatrist. Solicitor's J. 1981, 125, 89-91.

250. Benton, R.J. Film as dream: Alfred Hitchcock's Rear Window. Psychoanal Rev. 1984, 71, 483-500.

251. Beresford, H.R. The Quinlan decision: problems and legislative alternatives. Ann Neurol. 1977, 2, 74-81.

252. Berg & Fox. Factors in homicide committed by 200 males. J Social Psychol. 1947, 26, 109-119.

253. Bergman, J. The tragic story of two highly gifted, genius-level boys. Creat Child Adult Quart. 1979, 4, 222-233.

254. Berkman, A.S. The state of Michigan versus a battered wife. A case study. Bull Menninger Clin. 1980, 44, 603-16.

255. Berkovitz, I.H. Feelings of powerlessness and the role of violent actions in adolescents. Adoles Psychiat. 1981, 9, 477-492.

256. Berman, A.L. Dyadic death: murder-suicide. Suicide Life Threat Behav. 1979, 9, 15-23.

257. Berman, A.L. The epidemiology of life-threatening events. Suicide Life Threat Behav. 1975, 5, 67-77.

258. Berne, E. Cultural aspects of a multiple murder. Psychiat Quart Suppl. 1950, 24, 250, 269.

259. Bernstein, M.L. Two bite mark cases with inadequate scale references. J Forens Sci. 1985, 30, 958-64.

260. Bernstein, J.I. Premeditated murder by an eight-year old boy. Int J Offend Therap Comp Criminol. 1979, 23, 47-56.

261. Besharov, D.J. Protecting abused and neglected children: can law help social work? Child Abuse Negl. 1983, 7, 421-34.

262. Bessick, E.A. Gun control statutes and domestic violence. Cleve St Law Rev. 1970, 19, 556-567.

263. Beukenkamp, C. Phantom patricide. Arch Gen Psychiat. 1960, 3, 282-8.

264. Bhaskaran, C.S. Role of forensic pathologist in homicide investigation. J Ind Med. 1969, 52, 171-3.

265. Bhatt, K.K., Bhatt, Law & Chudger, M. A comparative study of the conflict level among the known maladjusted groups. Ind J Clin Psychol. 1976, 143-147.

266. Bierer, G.S. Love-making--an act of murder. The "Golem" syndrome. J Int J Soc Psychiat. 1976, 22, 197-9.

267. Biggs, J., Jr. The Guilty Mind: Psychiatry and the Law of Homicide. Johns Hopkins Univ Press, Baltimore, MD, 1967.

268. Biggs, J., Jr. The Guilty Mind: Psychiatry and the Law of Homicide. Harcourt Brace, N.Y. 1955.

269. Bjerre. The Psychology of Murder. Longmans, Green and Co., N.Y. 1927.

270. Black, T. & Orsagh, T. New evidence on the efficacy of sanctions as a deterrent to homicide. Soc Sci Quart. 1978, 58, 616-631.

271. Blackburn, R. Emotionality, extraversion and aggression in paranoid and nonparanoid schizophrenic offenders. Brit J Psychiat. 1968, 114, 1301-1302.

272. Blackman, N. & Lum, J.T., Vanderpearl, R.J. Disturbed communications: A contributing factor in sudden murder. Ment Hlth Soc. 1974, 1, 345-355.

273. Blackman, N., Weiss, J.M.A. and Lemberti, J.W. The sudden murderer: III. Clues to preventive interaction. Arch Gen Psychiat. 1963, 8, 289-294.

274. Blair, D. Homicide. Med Sci Law 1981, 2, 134-136.

275. Blake, L.W. The sentence for murder: The case for retribution. New Law J. 1973, 123, 862-864.

276. Blanks, R.C. Criminal law -- perfecting the imperfect right of self-defense. Campbell Law Rev. 1982, 2, 427-446.

277. Blaser, M.J., Jason, J.M., Weniger, B.G., Elsea, W.R., Finton, R.J., Hanson, R.A. & Feldman, R.A. Epidemiologic analysis of a cluster of homicides of children in Atlanta. JAMA, 1984, 251, 3255-8.

278. Blinder, M.G. The domestic homicide: II. Family Ther. 1985, 12, 1-24.

279. Blinder, M.G. The domestic homicide. Family Ther. 1984, 11, 185-198.

280. Blinn, K.W. First degree murder--A workable definition. J Crim Law Criminol. 1950, 40, 729-735.

281. Bloch, D. Fantasy and the fear of infanticide. Psychoanal Rev. 1974, 61, 5-31.

282. Block, C.R. Race/ethnicity & patterns of Chicago homicide 1965 to 1981. J Crime Delinq. 1985, 31, 104-116.

283. Block, R. Victim-offender dynamics in violent crime. J Crim Law Criminol. 1981, 72, 743-761.

284. Block, R. Victim and offender in violent crime. Victimology. 1977, 2, 55.

285. Block, R. Violent Crime. D.C. Heath and Company, Lexington, MA, 1977.

286. Block, R. Community, environment, and violent crime. Criminol. 1979, 17, 46-57.

287. Block, R. Homicide in Chicago: A nine-year study (1965-1973). J Crim Law Criminol. 1976, 66, 496-510.

288. Blom-Cooper, Law A miscarriage of justice--English style. Med Leg J. 1981, 49, 97-117.

289. Bloom, J.D. Aspects of violence reduction. Alaska Med. 1975, 17, 3-8.

290. Bloom, J.D. Patterns of Eskimo homicide. Bull Am Acad Psychiat Law. 1975, 3, 165-74.

291. Bloom, J.D. Forensic psychiatric evaluation of Alaska native homicide offenders. Int J Law Psychiat. 1980, 3, 163-71.

292. Bluestone, H. & Travin, S. Murder: the ultimate conflict. Am J Psychoanal. 1984, 44, 147-67.

293. Bluglass, R. The psychiatric assessment of homicide. Br J Hosp Med. 1979, 22, 368-73, 375-7.

294. Blumenfield, M., Glickman, L. Ten months experience with LSD users admitted to County Psychiatric Receiving Hospital. N.Y. St J Med. 1967, 67, 1849-1853.

295. Blumstein, A. On the racial disproportionality of United States' prison populations. J Crim Law Criminol. 1982, 73, 1259-1281.

296. Boag, T.J. Mental health of native peoples of the Arctic. Can Psychiat Assoc J. 1970, 15, 115-120.

297. Bock, E.W. & Webber, I.L. Social status and relational system of elderly suicides: A reexamination of the Henry Short thesis. Suicide Life Threat Behav. 1972, 2, 145-159.

298. Bogan, J. Homicidal poisoning by strychnine. J Forens Sci Soc. 1966, 6, 166-9.

299. Bohannan, P. African Homicide and Suicide. Princeton Univ Press, Princeton, N.J. 1960.

300. Bolton, R. The hypoglycemia-aggression hypothesis: Debate versus research. Current Anthropol. 1984, 25, 1-28.

301. Bolton, R. Aggression and hypoglycemia among the Qolla: A study in psychobiological anthropology. Ethnology. 1973, 12, 3, 227-258.

302. Bonkalo, A. Electroencephalography in criminology. Can Psychiat Assoc J. 1967, 12, 281-286.

303. Bonnichsen, R., et al. Poisoning by volatile compounds. II. Chlorinated allphatic hydrocarbons. J Forens Sci. 1966, 11, 414-27.

304. Bonnie, R.J., Showalter, C.R. & Roddy, Y. The spousal homicide syndrome: legal implications. Bull Am Acad Psychiat Law. 1980, 8, 431-44.

305. Bonnie, R.J., Showalter, C.R. & Roddy, V. The spousal homicide syndrome: legal implications. Am Acad Psych Law Bull. 1980, 4, 431-444.

306. Boor, M. Reduction in deaths by suicide, accidents, and homicide prior to United States presidential elections. J Soc Psychol 1982, 118, 135-6.

307. Boor, M. & Fleming, J.A. Reductions in suicide and accident levels prior to presidential elections are independent of unemployment effects. J Soc Psychol. 1984, 124, 119-121.

308. Boor, M. Reduction in deaths by suicide, accidents, and homicide prior to United States presidential elections. J Soc Psychol. 1982, 118, 135-136.

309. Borgman, R.D. Social Conflict and Mental Health Services. C.C. Thomas, Springfield, Ill., 1978.

310. Boris, S.B. Stereotypes and dispositions for criminal homicide. Criminol. 1979, 17, 139-58.

311. Boroch, R. Offender rehabilitation services and the defense of criminal cases: The Philadelphia experience. Crim Law Bull. 1971, 7, 215-224.

312. Boswell, C. & Thompson, L. Curriculum of Murder. Collier, N.Y., 1962.

313. Bottiger, L.E. The murderer's vade mecum. Br Med J [Clin Res]. 1982, 285, 1819-21.

314. Boudouris, J. Criminality and addiction. Int J Addict. 1976, 11, 951-966.

315. Boudouris, J. A classification of homicides. Criminol. 1974, 11, 525-540.

316. Boudouris, J. Homicide and the family. J Marr Fam. 1971, 33, 667-676.

317. Bowers, W.J. The pervasiveness of arbitrariness and discrimination under post-furman capital statutes. J Crim Law Criminol. 1983, 3, 1067-1100.

318. Bowker, L.H. The incidence of female crime and delinquency -- a comparison of official and self-report statistics. Int J Women's Stud. 1978, 1, 178-192.

319. Bowker, L.H. The criminal victimization of women. Victimology. 1979, 4, 371-384.

320. Bowman, P.J. Toward a dual labor-market approach to black-on-black homicide. Pub Hlth Rep. 1980, 95, 555-6.

321. Boyanowsky, E.O., Newtson, D. & Walster, E. Film preferences following a murder. Communicat Res. 1974, 1, 32-43.

322. Bradford, J.M. & Smith, S.M. Amnesia and homicide: the Padola case and a study of thirty cases. Bull Am Acad Psychiat Law. 1979, 7, 219-31.

323. Brahams, D. Premenstrual tension and criminal responsibility. Practitioner. 1983, 227, 807-13.

324. Braithwaite, J. & Braithwaite, V. The effect of income inequality and social democracy on homicide. Brit J Criminol. 1980, 20, 1, 45-53.

325. Bramblet, H.H. Character of deceased and uncommunicated threats by deceased in homicide cases. Ky Law J. 1943, 32, 84-6.

326. Brandt, A.A., Walshon, J. & Kelly, J.J. Drunken injured drivers: are they "getting away with murder"? Conn Med. 1985, 49, 377-9.

327. Brass, A. When doctors disagree. Br J Hosp Med. 1982, 28, 238.

328. Braucht, G.N., Loya, F. & Jamieson, K.J. Victims of violent death: a critical review. Psychol Bull. 1980, 87, 309-33.

329. Brearley, H.C. & Patterson, S. Homicide in the United States. Patterson Smith, New Jersey, 249.

330. Brearley, H.C. Homicide in the United States. Univ North Carolina Press, Chapel Hill, 1932.

331. Brearley, H.C. Firearms and homicide. Soc Social Res. 1931. 15, 456-62.

332. Brearley, H.C. The negro and homicide. Soc Forces. 1930, 9, 247-253.

333. Brearley, H.C. Homicide in South Carolina: a regional study. Soc Forces. 1929, 8, 218-21.

334. Brenner, M.H. Health costs and benefits of economic policy. Int J Hlth Serv. 1977, 7, 581-623.

335. Brenner, M.H. Mortality and economic instability: detailed analyses for Britain and comparative analyses for selected industrialized countries. Intern J Hlth Serv. 1983, 13, 563-620.

336. Brenner, M.H. Personal stability and economic security. Soc Pol. 8, 2-4, 1977.

337. Brett, P. The law and the changing view of man. Aust N Zeal J Psychiat. 1971, 5, 78-83.

338. Brewer, C. Homicide during a psychomotor seizure. Med J Aust. 1971, 2, 730-731.

339. Brewer, C. Murder and the McNaughten rules: The importance of adequate medical investigation. Aust N Zeal J Criminol. 1971, 4, 94-100.

340. Brewer, J.R. Homicide: felony-murder rule -- a new test in Kansas for inherently dangerous collateral felonies. Washburn Law J. 1981, 3, 646-651.

341. Brinkmann, B., Fechner, G. & Puschel, K. Identification of mechanical asphyxiation in cases of attempted masking of the homicide. Forens Sci Int. 1984, 26, 235-45.

342. Brittain, R.P. The sadistic murderer. Med Sci Law. 1970, 10, 198-207.

343. Brittain, R.P. Cruentations in legal medicine and in literature. Med Hist. 1965, 9, 82-8.

344. Brock, J.C. Drunken driving and murder. Ky Law J. 1947, 36, 138-41.

345. Brodie, D.W. The new biology and the prenatal child. J Fam Law. 1970, 9, 4, 391-407.

346. Brody, M. Trial of Daniel M'Naughten. Insanity defense, and its well-kept secret. N.Y. St J Med. 1982, 82, 381-6.

347. Bromberg, W. The Mold of Murder: A Psychiatric Study of Homicide. Grune & Stratton, New York, 1961.

348. Bromberg, W. The Mold of Murder: A Psychiatric Study of Homicide. Greenwood Press, Connecticut, 1961.

349. Bromberg, W. A psychological study of murder. Int J Psychoanal. 1951, 32, 117-127.

350. Brophy, J. The Meaning of Murder. Thomas Y. Crowell Co., N.Y., 1966.

351. Broudy, D.W. & May, P.A. Demographic and epidemiologic transition among the Navajo Indians. Soc Biol. 1983, 30, 1-16.

352. Brown, B. Murderous intent and the "lesser offenses." N Zeal Law J. 1965, 1965, 537.

353. Brown, C.L. Motivations in murder. J Med Assoc State Ala. 1980, 49, 11-2, 17-20.

354. Brown, K.A. The identification of Linda Agostini: the significance of dental evidence in the Albury Pyjama Girl case. Am J Forens Med Pathol. 1982, 3, 131-41.

355. Browne, W.J. & Palmer, A.J. A preliminary study of schizophrenic women who murdered their children. Hosp Commun Psychiat. 1975, 26, 71, 75.

356. Browning, C.H. Handguns and homicide: a public health problem. JAMA. 1976, 236, 2198-2200.

357. Brownlie, A.R. Evidence - statements by suspect to police-admissibility. Crim Law Rev. 1981, 782-783.

358. Brozovsky, M. and Falit, H. Neonaticide: Clinical and psychodynamic considerations. J Am Acad Child Psychiat. 1971, 10, 673-683.

359. Brunn, J.T. Retrograde amnesia in a murder suspect. Amer J Clin Hypn. 1968, 10, 209-13.

360. Buchan, T. Some clinical and cultural correlates of violent death. S Afr Med J. 1978, 54, 536-40.

361. Buchanan, E.C. Three Years of Murder. Dutton, N.Y., 1979.

362. Buchanan, P.H., Jr. Courting disaster. Recollections of an Indiana judge about Dr. E. Rogers Smith. Indiana Med. 1985, 78, 660.

363. Buckhout, R., Weg, S., Reilly, V. and Frohboese, R. Jury verdicts: comparison of 6- vs. 12-person juries and unanimous vs. majority decision rule in a murder trial. Bull Psychon Soc. 1977, 10, 175-179.

364. Buda, M.A. & Butler, T.L. The battered wife syndrome: A backdoor assault on domestic violence. Soc Action Law. 1985, 10, 63-71.

365. Budd, R.D. The incidence of alcohol use in Los Angeles County homicide victims. Am J Drug Alc Abuse. 1982, 9, 105-11.

366. Budd, R.D. & Lindstrom, D.M. Characteristics of victims of PCP-related deaths in Los Angeles County. J Toxicol Clin Toxicol. 1982, 19, 997-1004.

367. Bugliosi, V. & Gentry, C. Helter Skelter. Bantam, N.Y., 1975.

368. Bugliosi, V. Helter Skelter: The True Story of Manson Murders. Norton, N.Y., 1974.

369. Bulhan, H.A. Black psyches in captivity and crises. Race and Class. 1979, 20, 243-261.

370. Bullock, H.A. Urban homicide in theory and fact. J Crim Law Criminol Pol Sci. 1955, 45, 565-575.

371. Burchell, H.B. Digitalis poisoning: historical and forensic aspects. J Am Coll Cardiol. 1983, 1, 506-16.

372. Burgess, A.W. Family reaction to homicide. Am J Orthopsychiat. 1975, 45, 391-398.

373. Burgess, A. Community Mental Health: Target Populations. Prentice Hall, Englewood Cliffs, NJ, 1976.

374. Burka, E.R. Was "Murder in Guatemala" inappropriate? N Engl J Med. 1984, 31, 337-8.

375. Bursten, B. Isolated violence to the loved one. Bull Am Acad Psychiat Law. 1981, 9, 116-27.

376. Bursten, B. Voluntariness of waiver of fifth amendment rights. Bull Am Acad Psychiat Law. 1979, 7, 352-62.

377. Burton, B.B.G. The amok syndrome in Papua and New Guinea. Med J Aust. 1968, 1, 252-6.

378. Burton, R. Relationship of lunar phase to homicide occurrence./The moon murderers. World Med. 1972, 8, 37, 39, 41.

379. Butler, J.R., Trice, J., Calhoun, K. Diagnostic significance of the tattoo in psychotic homicide. Correct Psychiat J Soc Ther. 1968, 14, 110-113.

380. Butts, S.W. Criminal law (annual survey of Texas law). SW Law J. 1981, 1, 493-525.

381. Buzawa, E.S. & Buzawa, C.G. Legislative responses to the problem of domestic violence in Michigan. Wayne Law Rev. 1979, 25, 859-881.

C

382. Caffey, J. The whiplash shaken infant syndrome: manual shaking by the extremities with whiplash-induced intracranial and intraocular bleedings, linked with residual permanent brain damage and mental retardation. Pediatrics. 1974, 54, 396-402.

383. Cain, S. The psychodynamics of the presidential assassin and an examination of the theme/graphic variables of his threatening correspondence. Forens Sci Int. 1982, 19, 39-50.

384. Cairns, F.J., Koelmeyer, T.D. & Smeeton, W.M. Deaths from drowning. NZ Med J. 1984, 97, 65-7.

385. Cameron, A.H. and Asher, P. Cot deaths in Birmingham 1958-61. Med Sci Law 1965, 5, 187.

386. Cameron, J.M. The Bible and legal medicine. Med Sci Law. 1970, 10, 7-13.

387. Cameron, J.M. Changing patterns in violence. Med Sci Law. 1973, 13, 261-4.

388. Cameron, R.G. Criminal law - subject of infanticide So Calif Law Rev. 1947, 20, 357-60.

389. Camp, J. The murderous Dr. Clements. Med Leg J. 1978, 46, 72-84.

390. Campbell, A.V. Viability and the moral status of the fetus. Ciba Found Symp. 1985, 115, 228-43.

391. Campbell, D.E. & Beets, J.L. Lunacy and the moon. Psychol Bull. 1978, 85, 1123-9.

392. Campion, J., Cravens, J.M., Rotholc, A., Weinstein, H.C., Covan, F. & Alpert, M. A study of 15 matricidal men. Am J Psychiat. 1985, 142, 312-7.

393. Camps, F. More about Jack the Ripper. Criminologist. 1968, 7, 12.

394. Camps, F. More about Jack the Ripper. Lond Hosp Gaz. 1966, 59, 1.

395. Camps, F.E. Causation in homicide -- a medical view. Harvard Crim Law Rev. 1957, 576.

396. Cantor, D. & Cohen, L.E. Comparing measures of homicide trends: methodological and substantive differences in the vital statistics and uniform crime report time series (1933-1975). Soc Sci Res. 1980, 9, 2, 121-145.

397. Capote, T. In cold blood. Random, N.Y., 1966.

398. Cardarelli, A.P. An analysis of police killed by criminal action: 1961-1963. J Crim Law Criminol Pol Sci. 1968, 59, 447-453.

399. Carr, P.J. The Yorkshire Ripper case: not only was Peter Sutcliffe on trial! J Adv Nurse. 1982, 7, 173-7.

400. Carrington, P., Ephron, H.S. Moral Considerations in the Psychotherapy of an Adolescent who Attempted Murder. In: Post, S. (ed.) Moral Values and the Superego Concept in Psychoanalysis. International Universities Press, N.Y., 1972, 290-317.

401. Carroll, P.G. Commonwealth v. Cass. (whether viable fetus is a "person" within the meaning of the vehicular homicide statute). New Eng Law Rev. 1984, 2, 309-318.

402. Carter, W.B. Suicide, death, and ghetto life. Suicide Life Threat Behav. 1971, 1, 264-271.

403. Caryl, T.E. Emotional disturbance produced by terror - whether constituting "harm" in context of manslaughter. Crim Law Rev. 1985, 383-384.

404. Caryl, T.E. Causing death by reckless driving - tests to be applied - admissibility of evidence of consumption of alcohol. Crim Law Rev. 1984, 628-629.

405. Caryl, T.E. Joint enterprise - liability of each accomplice for facts of the other - murder committed in the course of robbery. Crim Law Rev. 1984, 616-617.

406. Caryl, T.E. Murder - defense of diminished responsibility. Crim Law Rev. 1982, 302-303.

407. Case, M.E., Poklis, A. & Mackell, M.A. Homicide by intravenous injection of naphtha. J Forens Sci. 1985, 30, 208-12.

408. Cassity, J.H. Personality study of 200 murderers. J Crim Psychopath. 1941, 2, 296-304.

409. Cassity, J.H. The Quality of Murder. Julian Press N.Y., 1958, 268.

410. Catton, J., Behind the Scenes of Murder. W.W. Norton & Company, N.Y., 1940, 355.

411. Cavanaugh, J.L., Rogers, R. & Wasyliw, O.E. A computerized assessment program for forensic science evaluations: a preliminary report. J Forens Sci. 1982, 27, 113-8.

412. Cebelin, M.S. & Hirsch, C.S. Human stress cardiomyopathy. Myocardial lesions in victims of homicidal assaults without internal injuries. Hum Pathol. 1980, 11, 123-32.

413. Center for Studies of Crime and Delinquency. Suicide, Homicide, and Alcoholism Among American Indians: Guidelines for Help. Department of Health Education and Welfare, 1973.

414. Centerwall, B.S. Race, socioeconomic status, and domestic homicide, Atlanta, 1971-72. Am J Publ Hlth. 1984, 74, 813-5.

415. Cerbus, G. Seasonal variation in some mental health statistics: suicides, homicides, psychiatric admissions and institutional placement of the retarded. J Clin Psychol. 1970, 26, 61-63.

416. Chao, T.C. Homicides and suspected homicides in Singapore. Med Sci Law. 1973, 13, 98-102.

417. Chapman, A. A double murder, the police investigation. J Forens Sci. 1964, 4, 124-9.

418. Chapman, J.L. Evaluation of psychological stress as an investigative tool. Leg Med. 1980, 57-74.

419. Charbonneau, L. The Grange report. Nurses criticize commission's report for lack of answers. Can Nurse. 1985, 81, 14-8.

420. Charny, I.W. A contribution to the psychology of genocide: sacrificing others to the death we fear ourselves. Israel Yearbook on Human Rights. 1980, 10, 90-108.

421. Check, W.A. Homicide, suicide, other violence gain interesting medical attention. JAMA. 1985, 254, 721-3, 727-8, 730.

422. Cheney, M. The co-ed killer: A study of the murders, mutilations, and matricide of Edmund Kemper III. Walker & Co., New York, 1976, 222.

423. Chetta, N.J., Medina, I., Jr., Sanchez, R.C., Comstock, A.P. and Andrews, D.B. The effects of alcohol in traumatic deaths. J Louis Med Soc. 1960, 112, 833-7.

424. Chilton, R. & Galvin, J. Race, crime and criminal justice. Crime Delinq. 1985, 31, 3-14.

425. Chimbos, P.D. Marital violence: a study of interspouse homicide. 1977, 37, 6081-A.

426. Chiswick, D. Insanity in bar of trial in Scotland: A state hospital study. Br J Psychiat. 1978, 132, 598-601.

427. Chiswick, D. Matricide. Br Med J [Clin Res]. 1981, 14, 1279-80.

428. Choi, S.Y. Death in young alcoholics. J Stud Alc. 1975, 36, 1224-1229.

429. Christison, R. Medicolegal contributions of historical interest. Case IV., Murder by suffocation. Forens Sci. 1972, 1, 119-31.

430. Christoffel, K.K., Zieserl, E.J. & Chiaramonte, J. Should child abuse and neglect be considered when a child dies unexpectedly? Am J Dis Child. 1985, 139, 876-880.

431. Christoffel, K.K. Homicide in childhood: a public health problem in need of attention. Am J Pub Hlth. 1984, 74, 68-70.

432. Christoffel, K.K., Anzinger, N.K. & Amari, M. Homicide in childhood. Distinguishable patterns of risk related to developmental levels of victims. Am J Forens Med Pathol. 1983, 4, 129-37.

433. Christoffel, K.K. & Liu, K. Homicide death rates in childhood in 23 developed countries: U.S. rates atypically high. Child Abuse Negl. 1983, 7, 339-45.

434. Christoffel, K.K., Liu, K. & Stamler, J. Epidemiology of fatal child abuse: international mortality data. J Chronic Dis. 1981, 34, 57-64.

435. Chuck, D. Homicide and the neglect to obtain proper medical treatment. W Ind Law J. 1984, 2, 208-211.

436. Clark, J.G. Modern felony murder doctrine. Ky Law J. 1940, 28, 215-18.

437. Clark, T. & Penycate, J. Psychopath: The case of Patrick Mackay. Routledge & Kegan Paul, London, 1976.

438. Cleary, M.F. Dissociative reaction/temporal lob epilepsy: Psychiatric excuses in legal proceedings. Am J Forens Psychiat. 1985, 6, 30-37.

439. Cleary, M.F. Dissociative states: Disproportionate use as a defense in criminal proceedings. Am J Forens Psychiat. 1983, 4, 157-165.

440. Cleveland, F.P. Problems in homicide investigation. IV. The relationship of alcohol to homicide. Cincinnati J Med. 1955, 36, 28-30.

441. Cobb, S.F. An exploratory study of episodic violent behavior in selected groups of subjects. Diss Abs. 1974, 34, 6768-6769.

442. Cohen, B.J. Crime in America: Perspectives on criminal and delinquent behavior. F.E. Peacock, Itasca, Illinois, 1970.

443. Cohen, J. The geography of crime. Ann Am Acad Pol Soc Sci. 1941, 217, 29-37.

444. Cohen, L.H. Murder, Madness and the Law. World Pub. Co. England, 1952, 183.

445. Cohen, L.H. & Coffin, T.E. Pattern of murder in insanity; a criterion of the murderer's abnormality. J Crim Law. 1946, 37, 262-87.

446. Cohen, M.E. The "brave new baby" and the law: fashioning remedies for the victims of in vitro fertilization. Am J Law Med. 1978, 4, 319-36.

447. Cohen, W.D. Heroin deaths: Homicidal responsibility of the seller in N.Y.. Albany Law Rev. 1973, 37, 497-523.

448. Cohn, M.S. The demise of the felony murder doctrine in Michigan. Wayne Law Rev. 1981, 1, 215-238.

449. Coid, J. The epidemiology of abnormal homicide and murder followed by suicide. Psychol Med. 1983, 13, 855-60.

450. Coid, J. Suggestibility, low intelligence and a confession to crime. Br J Psychiat. 1981, 139, 436-438.

451. Coid, J. How many psychiatric patients in prison? Br J Psychiat. 1984, 145, 78-86.

452. Coldiron, W.H. Historical development of manslaughter. Ky Law J. 1950, 38, 527-50.

453. Cole, K.E., Fisher, G., Cole, S.S. Women who kill. A sociopsychological study. Arch Gen Psychiat. 1968, 19, 1-8.

454. Coleman, S. Intoxication in mitigation of murder. J Crim Law. 1940, 31, 72-7.

455. Collinson, J.G. The role of the investigating officer. J Forens Sci Soc. 1970, 10, 199-203.

456. Combs-Orme, T., Taylor, J.R., Scott, E.B. & Holmes, S.J. Violent deaths among alcoholics. A descriptive study. J Stud Alc. 1983, 44, 938-49.

457. Connor, H.E., Daggett, Law, Maris, R.W., Weiss, S. Comparative psychopathology of suicide attempts and assaults. Suicide Life Threat Behav. 1973, 3, 33-50.

458. Connor, W.D. Criminal homicide, USSR/USA: Reflections on Soviet data in a comparative framework. J Crim Law Criminol. 1973, 64, 111-117.

459. Constantino, J.P. An epidemiologic study of homicides in Allegheny County, Pennsylvania. Am J Epidemiol. 1977, 106, 314-324.

460. Conley, J. M. Criminal law - Michigan Supreme Court abrogates common law felony-murder rule. (case note). Suffolk Univ Law Rev. 1981, 5, 1304-1323.

461. Cook, J.G. Offenses. (Criminal law in Tennessee in 1979 - A critical survey). Tenn Law Rev. 1980, 1, 3-18.

462. Cook, P.J. The effect of gun availability on violent crime patterns. Ann Am Acad Pol Soc Sci. 1981, 455, 63-79.

463. Cooper, R.J. Constructive manslaughter-meaning of "harm". J Crim Law 1985, 3, 225-228.

464. Cooper, R.J. Manslaughter by reckless driving. J Crim Law 1984, 1, 63-66.

465. Cooper, S.W. & Kimbrough, R.D. Acute dimethylintrosamine poisoning outbreak. J Forens Sci. 1980, 25, 874-82.

466. Copeland, A.R. Homicide in childhood. The Metro-Dade County experience from 1956 to 1982. Am J Forens Med Pathol. 1985, 6, 21-4.

467. Copeland, A.R. Dyadic death - revisited. J Forens Sci Soc. 1985, 3, 181-188.

468. Copeland, A.R. Death wearing a badge--a study of police officers who died in the line ot duty in Metro Dade County from 1956 to 1982. Forens Sci Int. 1984, 25, 175-9.

469. Copeland, A.R. Homicide during teenage years--the ten year Metro-Dade County experience from 1973 to 1982. Forens Sci Int. 1984, 25, 167-73.

470. Copeland, A.R. Deaths in custody revisited. Am J Forens Med Pathol. 1984, 5, 121-4.

471. Copeland, A.R. The right to keep and bear arms--a study of civilian homicides committed against those involved in criminal acts in metropolitan Dade County from between 1957 to 1982. J Forens Sci. 1984, 29, 584-90.

472. Corbett, M.E. & Spence, D. A forensic investigation of teeth marks in soap. Br Dent J. 1984, 157, 270-1.

473. Corder, B.F. Adolescent parricide: A comparison with other adolescent murder. Am J Psychiat. 1976, 133, 957-961.

474. Corder, J. The child, privileged victim of crimes of passion. Victimology. 1983, 8, 131-136.

475. Cordner, S.M. The Leicester case. Med J Aust. 1982, 1, 313-4.

476. Cormier, B.M. & Markus, B. A longitudinal study of adolescent murderers. Bull Am Acad Psychiat Law. 1980, 8, 240-60.

477. Cormier, B.M., Angliker, C.C.J., Boyer, R., Mersereau, G. The psychodynamics of homicide committed in a semispecific relationship. Can J Criminol Correct. 1972, 14, 335-344.

478. Cormier, B.M., Augliker, C.C.J., Boyer, R., Kennedy, M., Mersereau, G. The psychodynamics of homicide committed in a specific relationship. Can J Criminol Correct. 1971, 13, 1-8.

479. Cormier, B.M. On the history of man and genocide. Can Med Ass J. 1966, 94, 276-91.

480. Cormier, B.M. Psychodynamics of homicide committed in a marital relationship. Correct Psychiat J Soc Ther. 1962, 8, 187-194.

481. Cornelius, J.R., Soloff, P.H. & Reynolds, C.F., 3rd. Paranoia, homicidal behavior, and seizures associated with phenylpropanolamine. Am J Psychiat. 1984, 141, 120-1.

482. Corson, D. Lying and killing: language and the moral reasoning of twelve-and fifteen-year-olds by social group. Adolescence. 1984, 19, 473-82.

483. Corzine, J., Creech, J. & Corzine, L. Black concentration and lynchings in the south: Testing Blalock's power-threat hypothesis. Soc Forces. 1983, 61, 774-796.

484. Coser, L.A. Violence and the Social Structure. In: Palmer, S. (ed.) Rebellion and Retreat. Charles E. Merrill, Columbus, Ohio,1972.

485. Costello, R.M., Parsons-Manders, P. & Schneider, S.L. Alcoholic mortality: a 12-year follow-up. Am J Drug Alc Abuse. 1978, 5, 199-210.

486. Cotton, P.G., Bene-Kociemba, A. & Roses, S. Transfers from a general hospital psychiatric service to a state hospital. Am J Psychiat. 1980, 137, 230-3.

487. Couch, S., Noguchi, T.T. & Wright, J. Demonstrative evidence developed at the autopsy. Am J Forens Med Pathol. 1981, 2, 135-8.

488. Couch, V. Criminal law: justifiable homicide in defense of another: Oklahoma's anachronistic statute. Okla Law Rev. 1982, 1, 141-150.

489. Cournos, F. Staff reaction to an inpatient homicide. Hosp Commun Psychiat. 1985, 36, 664-6.

490. Covey, K.H. Murder vs. assault: Verdicts, legal attitudes, and attributions of mock jurors. Diss Abs. 1981, 42, 426.

491. Cowan, C.L., Thompson, W.C. & Ellsworth, P.C. The effects of death qualification on jurors' predisposition to convict and on the quality of deliberation. Law Hum Behav. 1984, 8, 1-2, 53-79.

492. Cowan, P. Criminal law -- affirmative defenses in the Washington Criminal Code. Wash Law Rev. 1976, 51, 953-980.

493. Cowley, D. Homicide - the problem of causation. J Crim Law 1984, 1, 42-44.

494. Cowley, D. Manslaughter by an indirect act. J Crim Law 1983, 4, 240-243.

495. Cowley, D. Constructive manslaughter - new limits. J Crim Law 1982, 4, 188-191.

496 . Cowper, F. Riches and rank. (the manslaughter case of Michael Telling). N.Y. Law J. 1984, 2.

497 . Cowper, F.H. Intention to cause serious bodily harm - whether sufficient mens rea. Crim Law Rev. 1981, 51-52.

498 . Craig, K.D., Wood, K. Autonomic components of observers' responses to pictures of homicide victims and nude females. J Exper Res Personal. 1971, 5, 304-309.

499 . Cox, M. 'I took a life because I needed one': psychotherapeutic possibilities with the schizophrenic offender-patient. Psychother Psychosom. 1982, 37, 96-105.

500 . Cramblett, H.G. The uses of and poisoning by the barbiturates. J Crim Law Criminol Pol Sci. 1952, 43, 390-395.

501 . Cravens, J.M., Campion, J., Rothoic, A., Covan, F. & Cravens, F.A. A study of 10 men charged with patricide. Am J Psychiat. 1985, 142, 1089-92.

502 . Creighton, S. Deaths from non-accidental injury in children. Br Med J. 1980, 281, 147.

503 . Crist, R.G. Criminal law - intoxication as a defense -- burden of proof. Dick Law Rev. 1948, 53, 61-2.

504 . Crompton, R. & Gall, D. Georgi Markov--death in a pellet. Med Leg J. 1980, 48, 51-62.

505 . Crook, R.R. Criminal law - homicide - removal of intravenous feeding line from vegetative, comatose patient at family's request is not murder. Cum Law Rev. 1985, 1, 225-237.

506 . Cullen, T. Autumn of Terror. Bodley Head Co., London, 1965.

507 . Curran, W.J. Law-medicine notes: the insanity defense in the Falkland Islands: a test of diminished responsibility. N Engl J Med. 1982, 307, 596-7.

508 . Curran, W.J. Legal psychiatry in Massachusetts: Another step forward. N Engl J Med. 1971, 284, 713-714.

509 . Curran, W.J. Medical quacks and murder with words. New Engl J Med. 1964, 270, 728.

510. Curran & Schilder. A constructive approach to the problems of childhood and adolescence. J Crim Psychopathol. 1940, 2, 125-142.

511. Curtis, L.A. Violence, Race and Culture. Lexington Books, Lexington, Ma, 1975.

512. Curtis, L.A. Victim precipitation and violent crime. Soc Probl. 1974, 21, 594-605.

D

513. Dadrian, V.N. Factors of anger and aggression in genocide. J Hum Relat. 1971, 19, 394-417.

514. Daley, R. To Kill a Cop. Crown, N.Y. 1976.

515. Dallas, D. Psychology in action: savagery, show and tell. Am Psychol. 1978, 33, 388-390.

516. Dalton, K. Cyclical criminal acts in premenstrual syndrome. Lancet. 1980, 2, 1070-1.

517. Daly, L. Family violence: A psychiatric perspective. J Irish Med Assoc. 1975, 68, 450-453.

518. Daly, M. & Wilson, M. Homicide and kinship. Am Anthropol. 1982, 84, 2, 372.

519. Daly, M., Wilson, M. & Weghorst, S.J. Male sexual jealousy. Ethol Sociobiol. 1982, 3, 1, 11-27.

520. Damio, W. Urge to Kill. Pinnacle Books, N.Y. 1974.

521. Damme, C. Infanticide: The worth of an infant under law. Med Hist. 1978, 22, 1-24.

522. Dancoff, J. Murder in Los Angeles: a casebook of unsolved crime. L A Law. 1982, 10, 18-26.

523. Daniel, A.E. & Harris, P.W. Female homicide offenders referred for pre-trial psychiatric examination: a descriptive study. Bull Am Acad Psychiat Law. 1982, 10, 261-9.

524. Daniels and Gilula. Criminal Homicide and Assault. In: C.R. Bartol (ed.) Criminal Behavior: A Psychosocial Approach. Prentice-Hall, Inc. Englewood Cliffs, NJ. 1980, 208.

525. Danto, B.L. A psychiatric view of another survivor of homicide. The cop who kills. Am J Forens Med Pathol. 1984, 5, 257-63.

526. Danto, B.L. and Others. Crisis intervention in a classroom regarding the homicide of a teacher. School Counselor. 1978, 26, 69-102.

527. Danto, B.L. Firearms and violence. Intern J Offend Ther. 1979, 23, 135-146.

528. Danto, B.L. Firearm homicide in the home setting. Omega. 1970, 1, 331-347.

529. Danto, B.L. New frontiers in the relationship between suicidology and law enforcement. Suicide Life Threat Behav. 1979, 9, 195-204.

530. Danto, B.L. Suicide among murderers. Intern J Offend Ther. 1978, 22, 140-148.

531. Danto, B. Firearms and their role in homicide and suicide. Suicide Life Threat Behav. 1971, 1, 10-17.

532. Danto, B.L. The psychiatrist and violent death investigation. Am J Forens Med Pathol. 1982, 3, 29-33.

533. Danto, B.L. Patients who murder their psychiatrists. Am J Forens Psychiat. 1982-83, 3, 120-134.

534. Darbyshire, P. Infanticide: Lambs to the slaughter. Nurs Times. 1985, 81, 32-5.

535. Darity, W.A. Family planning, race consciousness and the fear of race genocide. Am J Publ Hlth. 1972, 62, 1454-9.

536. Das-Gupta, S.M. & Tripathi, C.B. Medicolegal autopsies in India. Delay and nonperformance--adverse effects. Am J Forens Med Pathol. 1984, 5, 79-82.

537. David, D.B. Homicide in American Fiction, 1798-1860: A Study in Social Values. Cornell Univ Press, Ithaca, 1968.

538. Davidson, G.M. Medico-legal aspects of infanticide. J Crim Psychopath. 1941, 2, 500-511.

539. Davidson, P.O. & Neufeld, R.W. Response to pain and stress: A multivariate analysis. J Psychosom Res. 1974, 18, 25-32.

540. Davis, D. Jack the Ripper--The handwriting analysis. Criminologist. 1974, 9, 62.

541. Davis, D.B. Homicide in American Fiction, 1798-1860: A Study in Social Values. Cornell Univ Press, Ithaca, NY, 1968.

542. Davis, J.H. Can sudden cardiac death be murder? J Forens Sci. 1978, 23, 384-387.

543. Davis, J.H. Alcohol as a precursor to violent death. J Drug Iss. 1975, 270-275.

544. Davis, J.H., Rao, V.J. & Valdes-Dapena, M. A forensic science approach to a starved child. J Forens Sci. 1984, 29, 663-9.

545. Davis, J.R. The human side of homicide. Fed Probat. 1984, 1, 70.

546. Davis, R. & Short, J.F., Jr. Dimensions of black suicide: A theoretical model. Suicide Life Threat Behav. 1978, 8, 161-173.

547. Davison, M.H. Medicine, murder and man. Medicoleg J. 1964. 32, 28-39.

548. Dawkins, M.P. Alcohol information on black Americans: Current status and future needs. J Alc Drug Educ. 1980, 5, 28-40.

549. Dawkins, M.P. Policy Issues. In: T.D. Watts. Black Alcoholism: Toward a Comprehensive Understanding. C.C. Thomas, Springfield, Ill. 1980, 206-220.

550. Dawson, E.B., Moore, T.D. & McGanity, W.J. Relationship of Lithium Metabolism to Mental Hospital Admission and Homicide. Dis Nerv Sys. 1972, 33, 546-556.

551. Day, L.H. Death from non-war violence: an international comparison. Soc Sci Med. 1984, 19, 917-27.

552. Decker, S.H. & Kohfeld, C.W. A deterrence study of the death penalty in Illinois, 1933-1980. J Crim Just. 1984, 12, 367-377.

553. Deford, M.A. Murderers Sane and Mad. Abelard, N.Y. 1965.

554. Defronzo, J. Climate and crime: Tests of an FBI assumption. Environ Behav. 1984, 16, 185-210.

555. Defronzo, J. Economic assistance to impoverished Americans: Relationship to incidence of crime. Criminology. 1983, 21, 119-136.

556. Dehaan, J.D. Homicide with a black powder handgun. J Forens Sci. 1983, 2, 468-481.

557. Deiker, T.E. A cross-validation of MMPI scales of aggression on male criminal criterion groups. J Consult Clin Psychol. 1974, 42, 196-201.

558. Deiker, T.E. Characteristics of males indicted and convicted of homicide. J Soc Psychol. 1974, 95, 151-152.

559. Deiker, T.E. WAIS characteristics of indicted male murderers. Psychol Rep. 1973, 32, 1066.

560. Dell, S. & Smith, A. Changes in the sentencing of diminished responsibility homicides. Br J Psychiat. 1983, 142, 20-34.

561. Del Tosto, D. The battered spouse syndrome as a defense to a homicide charge under the Pennsylvania Crimes Code. Vill Law Rev. 1980, 26, 105-134.

562. Demayo, A.V. & Gensheimer, L.K. "Ten years of homicides" -- a study of homicide defendants and victims in the New Haven county superior court between 1967 and 1977. Conn Bar J. 1979, 53, 516-29.

563. Demetriades, D. & van-der-Veen, B.W. Penetrating injuries of the heart: experience over two years in South Africa. J Trauma. 1983, 23, 1034-41.

564. Deming, J.E., Mittleman, R.E. & Wetli, C.V. Forensic science aspects of fatal sexual assaults on women. J Forens Sci. 1983, 28, 572-6.

565. Dennis, I.H. Manslaughter by omission. Current Legal Probl 1980, 255-267.

566. Dennis, R.E. Homicide among black males. Social costs to families and communities. Pub Hlth Rep. 1980, 95, 556-7.

567. Dennis, R.E. Social Stress and Mortality Among Nonwhite Males. Phylon. 1977, 38, 315-28.

568. DePorte, J.V. and Parkhurst, E. Homicide in New York State: A statistical study of the victims and criminals in thirty-seven counties in 1921-1930. Hum Biol. 1935, 7, 47-73.

569. Derham, E. How Could She Do That? A Study of the Female Criminal. Clarkson N. Potter, N.Y., 1969.

570. Deutsch, S.J. & Alt, F.B. The effect of Massachusetts' gun control law on gun-related crimes in the city of Boston. Eval Quart. 1977, 1, 543-568.

571. Devasia, V.V. & Devasia, L. Victim-offender relationship in female homicide by male: A study conducted in Maharashtra. J Soc Work. 1984, 45, 3, 317-324.

572. Devine, P.E. The Ethics of Homicide. Cornell Univ Press, Ithaca, 1978.

573. DeYoung, H. Homicide. Hum Behav. 1976, 5, 16-21.

574. Dhondt, W. & Vandewiele, M. Senegalese adolescents and the need to control theft and criminality. J Adoles. 1983, 6, 329-332.

575. Diamond, B.L. Murder and the death penalty: A case report. Am J Orthopsychiat. 1975, 45, 712-722.

576. Diamond, B.L. The psychiatrist as expert witness. Psychiat Clin North Am. 1983, 6, 597-609.

577. Diamond, B.L. The psychiatrist as advocate. J Psychiat Law. 1973, 1, 5-21.

578. Dicks, H.V. Licensed Massmurder; A Sociopsychological Study of Some SS Killers. Basic Books, N.Y., 1976.

579. Dickson, R.H. Causation in a Scottish homicide case. NZ Law J. 1981, 12, 415-417.

580. Dieckmann, E. Practical Homicide Investigation. C.C. Thomas, Springfield, Ill., 1961.

581. Dietz, M.L. Killing for Profit: The Social Organization of Felony Homicide. Nelson-Hall Pub., Chicago, IL, 1978.

582. Di-Maio, V.J. Trace evidence and the pathologist. Clin Lab Med. 1983, 3, 355-65.

583. Di-Maio, V.J. Rifle wounds from high velocity, center fire hunting ammunition. J Forens Sci. 1977, 22, 132-140.

584. Di-Maio, V.J. Homicidal death by air rifle. J Trauma. 1975, 15, 1034-7.

585. Di-Maio, V.J. A case of infanticide. J Forens Sci. 1974, 19, 744-754.

586. Dix, G.E. Participation by mental health professionals in capital murder sentencing. Int J Law Psychiat. 1978, 1, 283-308.

587. Doerner, W.G. A regional analysis of homicide rates in the United States. Criminology. 1975, 13, 90-101.

588. Doerner, W.G. Why does Johnny Reb die when shot? The impact of medical resources upon lethality. Sociol Inquiry. 1983, 53, 1-15.

589. Doerner, W.G. The violent world of Johnny Reb: An attitudinal analysis of the "Regional Culture of Violence" thesis. Sociol Forum. 1979, 2, 61-71.

590. Doerner, W.G. The index of southerness revisited: The influence of wherefrom upon whodunnit. Criminology. 1978, 16, 1, 47-56.

591. D'Orban, P.T. Women who kill their children. Br J Psychiat. 1979, 134, 560-571.

592. Dorpat, T.L. Suicide in murderers. Psychiat Dig. 1966, 27, 51-5.

593. Dowling, D.C. & Iscan, M.Y. Scientific evidence: a vital role in homicide cases. Trial. 1982, 9, 34-37.

594. Doyle, F.T. Marshalling of proofs in homicide cases. J Crim Law Criminol. 1946, 36, 473-484.

595. Drapkin, I., Viano, E. Victimology. Lexington Books, Lexington, Mass. 1974.

596. Dreher, R.H. Origin, development and present status of insanity as a defense to criminal responsibility in the common law. J Hist Behav Sci. 1967, 3, 47-57.

597. Dressler, J. Rethinking heat of passion: A defense in search of a rationale. J Crim Law Criminol. 1982, 73, 421-470.

598. Driver, E.D. Interaction and criminal homicide in India. Soc Forces. 1961, 40, 153-158.

599. Driver, M.V., West, L.R., Faulk, M. Clinical and EEG studies of prisoners charged with murder. Brit J Psychiat. 1974, 125, 583-587.

600. Drooz, R.B. Handguns and hokum: A methodological problem. JAMA. 1977, 238, 43-45.

601. Dube, K.C., Kumar, N. & Dube, S. "Makings of a dacoit". Int J Soc Psychiat. 1982, 28, 267-73.

602. Duh, R.W. & Asal, N.R. Mortality among laundry and dry cleaning workers in Oklahoma. Am J Pub Hlth. 1984, 74, 1278-80.

603. Duncan, G.M., Frazier, S.H., Litin, E.M., Johnson, A.M. and Barron, A.J. Etiological factors in first-degree murder. JAMA. 1958, 168, 29.

604. Duncan, J.W., Duncan, G.M. Murder in the family: A study of some homicidal adolescents. Am J Psychiat. 1971, 127, 1498-1502.

605. Dundee, J.W. Mysterious deaths at Ann Arbor. Anaesthesia. 1978, 33, 752-3.

606. Dunne, M. Drug intervention in the management of aggression and explosive behaviour. Aust Fam Phys. 1978, 7, 1442-8.

607. Dusseau, J.L. Tertium quid: a third something in a muddied puzzle. Perspect Biol Med. 1982, 25, 238-53.

608. Dutra, F.R. Electrical burns of the skin. Medicolegal investigation. Am J Forens Med Pathol. 1981, 2, 309-12.

609. Dutra, F.F. Medicolegal aspects of conflagrations. J Crim Law. 1949, 39, 771-7.

610. Dvoskin, J. Legal alternatives for battered women who kill their abusers. Bull Am Acad Psychiat Law. 1978, 6, 335-54.

E

611. Easson, W.M. Myxedema psychosis--insanity defense in homicide. J Clin Psychiat. 1980, 41, 316-8.

612. Easterlin, R.A. & Schapiro, M.O. Homicide and fertility rates in the United States: a comment. Soc Biol. 1979, 26, 341-3.

613. Eckert, W.G. The Whitechapel murders: the case of Jack the Ripper. Am J Forens Med Pathol. 1981, 2, 53-60.

614. Eckert, W.G. The Lindbergh case. A triumph in forensic investigation. Am J Forens Med Pathol. 1980, 1, 151-3.

615. Eckert, W.G. The murder masquerade. The Domer case. Am J Forens Med Pathol. 1980, 1, 71-2.

616. Eckert, W.G. The St. Valentine's Day Massacre. Am J Forens Med Pathol. 1980, 1, 67-70.

617. Eckert, W.G. Masquerade by inferno. J Florida Med Ass. 1966, 51, 963.

618. Edberg, S. The use of footprints for identification in infanticide: report of a case. J Forens Sci. 1965, 10, 225-31.

619. Edland, J.F. Homicide by barbiturates and alcohol. J Forens Sci. 1982, 27, 942-3.

620. Edwards, J. The homicide act, 1957: A critique. Br J Delinq. 1957, 8, 49-61.

621. Egger, S.A. A working definition of serial murder and the reduction of linkage blindness. J Pol Sci Admin. 1984, 12, 348-357.

622. Erickson, M.L. & Gibbs, J.P. Specific versus general properties of legal punishments and deterrence. Soc Sci Quart. 1975, 56, 390-397.

623. Erickson, M.L. & Gibbs, J.P. The deterrence question: Some alternative methods of analysis. Soc Sci Quart. 1973, 54, 534-551.

624. Erlanger, H.S. The empirical status of the subculture of violence thesis. Soc Probl. 1974, 22, 280-292.

625. Erlanger, H.S. Is there a "subculture of violence" in the south? J Crim Law Criminol. 1976, 66, 483-490.

626. Eth, S., Silverstein, S. & Pynoos, R.S. Mental health consultation to a preschool following the murder of a mother and child. Hosp Commun Psychiat. 1985, 36, 73-6.

627. Evans, C.M. Alcohol, violence and aggression. Br J Alc Alcohol. 1980, 15, 104-117.

628. Everett, P. Forensic pathology: a case for justice. Nurs Mirror. 1979, 149, 30-1.

629. Evseeff, G.S. A potential young murderer. J Forens Sci. 1976, 21, 441-50.

630. Evseeff, G.S. A psychiatric study of a violent mass murderer. J Forens Sci. 1972, 17, 371-6.

631. Ewing, C.P. "Dr. Death" and the case for an ethical ban on psychiatric and psychological predictions of dangerousness in capital sentencing proceedings. Am J Law Med. 1983, 8, 407-28.

632. Eyer, J. Prosperity as a cause of death. Int J Hlth Serv. 1977, 7, 125-150.

633. Eyre, D.P. A contribution to the understanding of the confusion of tongues. Int J Psychoanal. 1975, 56, 449-453.

F

634. Fabricant, J. Homicide in response to a threat of rape: a theoretical examination of the rule of justification. Golden Gate Univ Law Rev. 1981, 945-980.

635. Fairall, P. Murder - intoxication - common purpose. Crim Law J. 1984, 5, 339-340.

636. Fairall, P.A. Homicide - Tasmanian criminal code - provocation - objective element insanity-irresistible impulse. Crim Law J. 1982, 5, 248-268.

637. Fairbanks, D.N. & Fairbanks, G.R. Cocaine uses and abuses. Ann Plast Surg. 1983, 10, 452-7.

638. Falk, V.S. Roosevelt/Reagan--Schrank/ Hinckley. Wis Med J. 1982, 81, 9-10.

639. Farley, R. Homicide trends in the United States. Demography. 1980, 17, 177-88.

640. Farley, R. Homicide trends in the United States. Population. 1980, 35, 1224.

641. Farrell, R.A. & Swigert, V.L. Legal disposition of inter-group and intra-group homicides. Sociol Quart. 1978, 19, 565-576.

642. Farrell, W.C., Jr. & Dawkins, M.P. Determinants of genocide fear in a rural Texas community: a research note. Am J Pub Hlth. 1979, 69, 605-7.

643. Farrington, M.K. The seasonality of pathology: A sociological analysis. Diss Abs. 1981, 41, 4854-A.

644. Farson, D. Jack the Ripper. Michael Joseph, Ltd., London, 1972.

645 . Finnegan, P., McKinstry, E. & Robinson, G.E. Denial of pregnancy and childbirth. Can J Psychiat. 1982, 27, 672-4.

646 . Finney, J.C. Phases of psychopathology after assassination. Am J Psychiat. 1973, 130, 1379-80.

647 . Fischer, C.S. Spread of violent crime from city to countryside, 1955 to 1975. Rur Sociol. 1980, 45, 416-34.

648 . Fishbain, D.A., Rao, V.J. & Aldrich, T.E. Female homicide-suicide perpetrators -- A controlled study. J Forens Sci. 1985, 1148-1156.

649 . Fisher, F.L. A trial court may refuse to submit a "not guilty" verdict from the jury in a murder trial when the defendant has not denied that he committed the homicide, but has instead relied on an insanity defense. Ill Bar J. 1983, 2, 92-95.

650 . Fisher, J.C. Homicide in Detroit: the role of firearms. Criminology. 1976, 14, 387-400.

651 . Fisher, R.S. Alcohol, accidents and crime. Curr Med Digest. 1952, 19, 37-41.

652 . Flaherty, F.J. N.Y. lawyer slain; firm employee held. Nat Law J. 1982, 2.

653 . Flanagan, T.J. Correlates of institutional misconduct among state prisoners: A research note. Criminology. 1983, 21, 1, 29-39.

654 . Fletcher, S.M. Insulin. A forensic primer. J Forens Sci Soc. 1983, 23, 5-17.

655 . Foodman, A., Estrada, C. Adolescents who commit accidental homicide: the emotional consequence to the individual, family, and community. J Am Acad Child Psychiat. 1977, 16, 314-326.

656 . Foot, D. Ritual murder. Medicolegal J. 1959, 27, 103-13.

657 . Foote, J. Reliving Jonestown's horror: Larry Layton: Conspirator or scapegoat? Nat Law J. 1981, 8.

658 . Forbes, T.R. Early forensic medicine in England: the Angus murder trial. J Hist Med Allied Sci. 1981, 36, 296-309.

659 . Forbes, T.R. & Venes, J.L. The case of the quarrelsome watchmen. Trans Stud Coll Phys. 1979, 1, 58-61.

660 . Forbes, T.R. Inquests into London and Middlesex homicides, 1673-1782. Yale J Biol Med. 1977, 50, 207-20.

661 . Ford, A.B. & Rushforth, N.B. Urban violence in the United States--implications for health and for Britain in the future: discussion paper. J R Soc Med. 1983, 76, 283-8.

662 . Ford, A.B., Rushforth, N.B., Rushforth, N., Hirsh, C.S., Adelson, L. Violent death in a metropolitan county:II. changing patterns in suicides (1959-1974). Am J Pub Hlth. 1979, 69, 459-464.

663 . Ford, C.V., Castelnuovo, T.P., Goodman, S.J., Bustamante, J.P., Long, K. Chronic pain in a victim of attempted homicide. Int J Psychiat Med. 1974, 5, 283-293.

664 . Foreman, P. The physician's criminal liability for the practice of euthanasia. Baylor Law Rev. 1975, 27, 54-61.

665 . Forrest, T. The family dynamics of maternal violence. J Am Acad Psychoanal. 1974, 2, 215-230.

666 . Forst, B. Capital punishment and deterrence: conflicting evidence? J Crim Law Criminol. 1983, 74, 927-942.

667 . Fottrell, E. Violent behavior by psychiatric patients. Br J Hosp Med. 1981, 25, 28-32, 35, 37-38.

668 . Fox, R.H., Sr., Rimer, S., McCoy, M. & Evans, H.C. Search of the homicide scene. Leg Med. 1980, 21-9.

669 . Frame, C.B. Automobile deaths and involuntary manslaughter in West Virginia. West Law Rev. 1961, 63, 130.

670 . Franke, R.H., Thomas, E.W., Queenen, A.J. Suicide and homicide: common sources and consistent relationships. Soc Psychiat. 1977, 12, 149-156.

671 . Frankel, S. Beyond a Reasonable Doubt. Stein & Day, New York, 1971.

672. Frankel. One thousand murderers. J Crim Law Criminol. 1939, 29, 672-688.

673. Frayer, D.W. & Bridgens, J.G. Stab wounds and personal identify determined from skeletal remains: a case from Kansas. J Forens Sci. 1985, 30, 232-8.

674. Frazer, M. The female homicide victim: trends in a metropolitan county from 1969 to 1980. J Forens Sci. 1983, 28, 577-87.

675. Frazier, S.H. Principles of psychiatric emergency management. Curr Psychiat Ther. 1969, 9, 106-115.

676. Freed, H.M. & Gandell, R. Murder on the job: case report of a unique disaster. Ment Hlth Soc. 1979, 5, 231-40.

677. Freedman, J.L. Effect of television violence on aggressiveness. Psychol Bull. 1984, 96, 227-46.

678. Freeman, A.M. Gunshot wounds: initial assessment and management. Aust Nurses J. 1980, 10, 40-5.

679. Freeman, Law The "seeds" of murder as sown "in the nursery". Curr Iss Psychoanal Pract. 1984, 1, 19-28.

680. French, A.P. & Shechmeister, B.R. The multiple personality syndrome and criminal defense. Bull Am Acad Psychiat Law. 1983, 11, 17-25.

681. Fridman, G.H.L. Onus of proof in cases of murder. Crim Law Rev. 1959, 557.

682. Friedman, I.M. Alcohol and unnatural deaths in San Francisco youths. Pediatrics. 1985, 76, 191-3.

683. Friedman, S., Margolis, R., David, O.J. & Kesselman, M. Predicting psychiatric admission from an emergency room. Psychiatry, psychosocial, and methodological factors. J Nerv Ment Dis. 1983, 171, 155-8.

684. Friedrich, P. Assumptions underlying tarascan political homicide. Psychiat. 1962, 25, 315-327.

685. Fullerton, A.G. Necrophilia, murder and high intelligence. Br J Psychiat. 1978, 133, 382-3.

686. Furneaux, R. Medical Murderer. Abelard, N.Y. 1967.

G

687. Gabrielli, W.F. Urban environment, genetics, and crime. Criminology. 1984, 22, 645-652.

688. Gallagher, R.P., Threlfall, W.J., Spinelli, J.J. & Band, P.R. Occupational mortality patterns among British Columbia farm workers. J Occup Med. 1984, 26, 906-8.

689. Gallemore, J.L., Jr. "Motiveless" public assassins. Bull Am Acad Psychiat Law. 1976, 4, 51-7.

690. Galvin, J. Rape: a decade of reform. J Crime Delinq. 1985, 2, 163-168.

691. Galvin, J.A. & Macdonald, J.M. Psychiatric study of a mass murderer. Am J Psychiat. 1959, 115, 1057-61.

692. Gandossy, R.P., Williams, J.R., Cohen, J. & Harwood, H.J. Drugs and Crime: A survey and analysis of the literature. U.S. Department of Justice, National Institute of Justice. 1980.

693. Gansau, H. & Becker, U. Semi-automatic detection of gunshot residue (GSR) by scanning electron microscopy and energy dispersive X-ray analysis (SEM/EDX). Scan Electron Microsc. 1982, 107-14.

694. Gardiner, M. The Deadly Innocents: Portraits of Children who Kill. Basic Books, New York, 1976.

695. Garey, R.E. PCP (phencyclindine): an update. J Psyched Drugs. 1979, 11, 265-75.

696. Garey, R.E., Daul, G.C., Jr., Samuels, M.S. & Egan, R.R. Medical and sociological aspects of T`s and blues abuse in New Orleans. Am J Drug Alc Abuse. 1982-83, 9, 171-82.

697. Geller, J.L. & Appelbaum, P.S. Competency to stand trial: neuroleptic medication and demeanor in court. Hosp Commun Psychiat. 1985, 36, 6-7.

698. Gerber, P. Brain death, murder and the law. Med J Aust. 1984, 536-537.

699. Gerber, P. Impeaching medical evidence - causation and the law of homicide. Aust Law J. 1983, 7, 407-415.

700. Gerson, L.W. Alcohol-related acts of violence: Who was drinking and where the acts occurred. J Stud Alc. 1978, 7, 1294-1296.

701. Gettler, A.O. & Tiber, S. Quantitative determination of ethyl alcohol in human tissues. Arch Pathol. 3, 78-83.

702. Getzel, G.S. & Masters, R. Serving families who survive homicide victims. Soc Casework. 1984, 65, 138.

703. Gibbens, T.C.N. Sane and insane homicide. J Crim Law 1958, 49, 110.

704. Gibbs, T., Alexander, G.R. & Massey, R.M. Homicide in the elderly population in South Carolina, 1970-1979. J SC Med Assoc. 1984, 80, 25-7.

705. Gilbert, J.N. A study of the increased rate of unsolved criminal homicide in San Diego, California and its relationship to police investigative effectiveness. Am J Pol Sci. 1983, 2, 149-166.

706. Gillies, H. Homicide in the west of Scotland. Br J Psychiat. 1976, 128, 105-127.

707. Gillies, H. Murder in the west of Scotland. Br J Psychiat. 1965, 111, 1087-94.

708. Gillin, J.C. & Ochberg, F.M. Firearms Control and Violence. In: Daniels, D. (ed). Violence and the Struggle for Existence. Little, Brown, Boston, 1970, 241-255.

709. Gillin, J.L. Social backgrounds of sex offenders and murderers. Soc Forces. 1935, 14, 232-9.

710. Gilula, M.F., Daniels, D.N. Violence and man's struggle to adapt. Science. 1969, 164, 396-405.

711. Given, J.B. Society and Homicide in Thirteenth-Century England. Stanford Univ. Press, Stanford, 1977.

712. Glaser, D. A response to Bailey: more evidence on capital punishment as correlate of tolerance for murder. J Crime Delinq. 1976, 22, 40-43.

713. Glass, R.T., Andrews, E.E. & Jones, K., 3rd. Bite mark evidence: a case report using accepted and new techniques. J Forens Sci. 1980, 25, 638-45.

714. Glasser, M., Amdur, M.J. & Backstrand, J. The impact of psychotherapists and primary physicians on suicide and other violent deaths in a rural area. Can J Psychiat. 1985, 30, 195-202.

715. Gluckman, L. Kerempa: The psychodynamics of a 19th century murder. N Z Med J. 1964, 63, 486-91.

716. Goddard, C.H. A history of firearms identification to 1930. Am J Forens Med Pathol. 1980, 1, 155-68.

717. Godwin, J. Murder USA: The Ways We Kill Each Other. Ballantine Books, New York. 1978.

718. Gold, A.D. Homicide - first degree murder. Crim Law Quart. 1985, 3, 287-290.

719. Gold, A.D. Homicide - violent distinction of deceased - expert testimony - self-defence. Crim Law Quart. 1982, 2, 170-175.

720. Gold, A.D. Self-defence - excessive force. Crim Law Quart. 1981, 3, 329-334.

721. Gold, A.D. Insanity - diminished capacity. Crim Law Quart. 1981, 3, 326-329.

722. Gold, L.H. Invitation to homicide. J Forens Sci. 1965, 10, 415-21.

723. Goldenring, J.M. On homicide in children and adolescents. Am J Pub Hlth. 1984, 74, 623-4.

724. Goldfeld, A.E. Murder in Guatemala. N Engl J Med. 1984, 310, 1186.

725. Goldney, R.D. Homicide and suicide by aircraft. Forens Sci Int. 1983, 21, 161-3.

726. Goldney, R.D. Medical responsibility in murder and suicide. Med J Aust. 1979, 1, 50-1.

727. Goldstein, R.L. Those who kill without thinking. Am J Psychiat. 1972, 129, 766-7.

728. Goldstein, S. Impulse control. J Psychiat Nurs Ment Hlth Serv. 1976, 14, 36-40.

729. Goode, W. Violence Among Intimates. In: Mulvihill, D. (ed) Crimes of Violence, Government Printing Office, Washington 1969, 941-97.

730. Goodwin, D.W. Alcohol in suicide and homicide. Quart J Stud Alc. 1973, 34, 144-156.

731. Goodwin, D.W., Guze, S.B., Robins, E. Follow-up studies in obsessional neurosis. Arch Gen Psychiat. 1969, 20, 182-187.

732. Goodwin, D.W. Alcohol in Studies and Homicides. National Institute of Mental Health (DHEW), Bethesda, MD, 1972.

733. Goodwin, D.W. Follow-up studies in obsessional neurosis. Arch Gen Psychiat. 1969, 20, 182-187.

734. Goonetilleke, U.K. Two unusual cases of suicide by hanging. Forens Sci Int. 1984, 26, 247-53.

735. Gopalakrishnan, C.B. Homicide and forensic medicine. Ind J Appl Psychol. 1969, 6, 103-107.

736. Gordon, M.A. & McClure, R.M. How judgments of responsibility are affected by objective and subjective communications. J Forens Psychol. 1972, 4, 4-10.

737. Gorwitz, K., Bahn, A., Warthen, F.J., Cooper, M. Some epidemiological data on alcoholism in Maryland; based on admissions to psychiatric facilities. Quart J Stud Alc. 1970, 31, 423-443.

738. Gorwitz, K., Dennis, R. On the decrease in the life expectancy of Black males in Michigan. Pub Rep. 1976, 91, 141-145.

739. Gottschalk, L.A., McGuire, F.L., Heiser, J.F., Dinovo, E.C. & Birch, H. Drug abuse deaths in nine cities: a survey report. NIDA Res Monogr Ser. 1979, 29, 1-172.

740. Gottschalk, L.A., McGuire, F.L., Heiser, J.F., Dinovo, E.C. & Birch, H. A review of psychoactive drug-involved deaths in nine major United States cities. Int J Addict. 1979, 14, 735-58.

741. Gowda, B.C. A bolt as a projectile: report of a case. Forens Sci. 1972, 1, 107-9.

742. Grando, R. An approach to family crisis intervention. Fam Ther. 1975, 2, 201-214.

743. Grant, B.C. "Till death us do part": A social psychological analysis of women who kill their spouses. Diss Abs. 1983, 44, 871.

744. Grant, B.L., Coons, D.J. Guilty verdict in a murder committed by a veteran with post-traumatic stress disorder. Bull Am Acad Psychiat Law. 1983, 11, 355-358.

745. Gray, L.N. & Martin, J.D. Punishment and deterrence: Another analysis of Gibbs' data. Soc Sci Quart. 1969, 50, 389-395.

746. Greaves, G.B., Currie, J.S. & Carter, A.C. Atlanta, psychology, and the second siege: report to APA by the Georgia Psychological Association's ad hoc Resource Committee on Murdered and Missing Atlanta Children. Am Psychol. 1982, 37, 559-568.

747. Green, C.M. Filicidal impulses as an anniversary reaction to childhood incest. Am J Psychother. 1982, 36, 264-71.

748. Green, C.M. Matricide by sons. Med Sci Law. 1981, 21, 207-14.

749. Green, E., Wakefield, R.P. Patterns of middle and upper class homicide. J Crim Law Criminol. 1979, 70, 172-181.

750. Green, G.S. & Good, R. Homicide by use of a pellet gun. Am J Forens Med Pathol. 1982, 3, 361-5.

751. Green, M.A. Practical homicide investigation. J Sci Soc. 1984, 5, 530-531.

752. Green, T.A. Societal concepts of criminal liability for homicide in mediaeval England. Speculum. 1972, 47, 669-94.

753. Greenberg, S.W. Crime and addiction: an empirical analysis of the literature, 1920-1973. Contemp Drug Probl. 1974, 3, 221-270.

754. Greene, J.E. & Moore, J. & Staton, T. Inferences concealing the motivations of a murderer: A psychological study of "displaced" aggression. Am Psychol. 1948, 3, 335.

755. Greene, J.J. Macbeth: Masculinity as murder. Am Imago. 1984, 41, 155-180.

756. Greenland, C. Evaluation of violence and dangerous behavior associated with mental illness. Seminars Psychiat. 1971, 3, 345-356.

757. Greenlaw, J. Hospital responsibilities to the general public. Nurs Law Ethics. 1981, 2, 5,7.

758. Greenwald, G.I. & Greenwald, M.W. Medicolegal progress in inquests of felonious deaths: Westminster, 1761-1866. J Leg Med. 1981, 2, 193-264.

759. Griffitt, W. & Jackson, T. Simulated jury decisions: The influence of jury-defendant attitude similarity-dissimilarity. Soc Behav Personal. 1973, 1, 1-7.

760. Grinnell, F.W. Drunkenness and manslaughter -- should the Commonwealth have an appeal on certain questions of law in criminal cases? Mass Law Quart 1937, 22, 23-4.

761. Gross, S.R. & Mauro, R. Patterns of death--an analysis of racial disparities in capital sentencing and homicide victimization. Stanford Law Rev. 1984, 1, 27-153.

762. Groves, R.E. Is abortion murder: Nurs Times. 1972, 68, 624-5.

763. Grunberg, F., Klinger, B.I. & Grumet, B.R. Homicide and community-based psychiatry. J Nerv Ment Dis. 1978, 166, 868-74.

764. Grunberg, F., Klinger, B.I., Grumet, B. Homicide and deinstitutionalization of the mentally ill. Am J Psychiat. 1977, 134, 685-687.

765. Grunhut, M. Statistics in criminology. J Roy Stat Soc, Series A. 1951, 114, 139-162.

766. Gudjonsson, G.H. & Mackeith, J.A. A specific recognition deficit in a case of homicide. Med Sci Law. 1983, 23, 37-40.

767. Gudjonsson, G.H. & Petursson, H. Psychiatric court reports in Iceland 1970-1982. Acta Psychiatr Scand. 1984, 70, 44-9.

768. Gudjonsson, G.H. & Petursson, H. Some criminological and psychiatric aspects of homicide in Iceland. Med Sci Law. 1982, 22, 91-8.

769. Gulotta, G. Victimization and interpersonal misunderstandings in dyadic systems. Victimology. 1980, 5, 110-114.

770. Gunasekara, N.D. Infanticide in Ceylon. Ceylon Med J. 1956, 3, 140-163.

771. Gunasekara, N.D. Homicide in Ceylon. Ceylon Med. J. 1956, 3, 140-163.

772. Gunby, P. 'Sexual behavior in an abnormal situation. JAMA. 1981, 245, 215, 219.

773. Gunn, J. Epileptic homicide: a case report. Brit J Psychiat. 1978, 132, 510-513.

774. Gupta, S.M., Chandra, J. & Dogra, T.D. Blunt force lesions related to the heights of a fall. Am J Forens Med Pathol. 1982, 3, 35-43.

775. Gupta, S.M. & Srivastava, S.C. Psychosocial factors in homicidal behaviour. Ind J Clin Psychol. 1977, 4, 25-32.

776. Gustin, A.C. A police officer reacts. J Soc Iss. 1975, 31, 1, 211-215.

777. Guttmacher, M.S. The Mind of the Murderer. Farrar, Straus, and Cudahy, New York, 1960.

778. Guze, S.B., Goodwin, D.W. and Crane, J.B. Criminality and psychiatric disorders. Arch Gen Psychiat. 1969, 20, 583-591.

H

779. Haberman, P.W. & Baden, M.M. Alcohol, Other Drugs and Violent Death. Oxford Univ. Press, New York, 1978.

780. Haberman, P.W. & Baden, M.M. Alcoholism and violent death. Quart J Stud Alc. 1974, 35, 221-231.

781. Haddad, J.B. Allocation of burdens in murder-voluntary manslaughter cases: an affirmative defense approach. Chi Kent Law Rev. 1982, 1, 23-66.

782. Hagman, H.C. The history of dentures, Part II. The murder of Josiah Bacon. Dent Lab Rev. 1979, 54, 22-6.

783. Hahn, J.K., McKenney, H.C. Legally Sane. Resnery, Chicago, 1972.

784. Haines, J. Women, the law, and provocation. Aust Nurs J. 1981, 10, 1, 3.

785. Hair, P.E.H. Deaths from violence in Britain: A tentative secular survey. Pop Stud. 1971, 25, 5-24.

786. Haith, L.R. "An eye for an eye.": the need for sentencing guidelines in Michigan. Det C Law Rev. 1985, 2, 589-604.

787. Halpern, A.L. Further comments on the insanity defense in the aftermath of the Hinckley trial. Psychiatr Quart. 1984, 56, 62-9.

788. Halpern, A.L. Elimination of the exculpatory insanity rule. A modern societal need. Psychiatr Clin North Am. 1983, 6, 611-27.

789. Harm, T. & Rajs, J. Types of injuries and interrelated conditions of victims and assailants in attempted and homicidal strangulation. Forens Sci Int. 1981, 18, 101-23.

790. Harno, E. Some significant developments in criminal law and procedure in the last century. J Crim Law Criminol Pol Sci. 1951, 42, 427-467.

791. Harper, F.D., Dawkins, M.P. Alcohol abuse in the Black community. Black Scholar. 1977, 8, 23-31.

792. Harper, F.D. Research and treatment with black alcoholics. Alc Hlth Res Wld. 1980, 4, 10-16.

793. Harper, F.D. Alcohol use and alcoholism among black Americans: A review. In: T.D. Watts (ed). Black Alcoholism: Toward a Comprehensive Understanding. C.C. Thomas, Springfield, Ill., 1980.

794. Harries, K.D. The historical geography of homicide in the U.S., 1935-1980. Geoforum. 1985, 1, 73-83.

795. Harries, K.D., Stadler, S.J. and Zdorkowski, R.T. Seasonality and assault: Explorations in inter-neighborhood variation, Dallas 1980. Ann Assoc Am Geog. 1984, 74, 590-604.

796. Harries, K.D. & Stadler, S.J. Determinism revisited: Assault and heat stress in Dallas, 1980. Environ Behav. 1983, 15, 235-256.

797. Harris, J.E., Pontius, A.A. Dismemberment murder: In search of the object. J Psychiat Law. 1975, 3, 7-23.

798. Harris, R.D. Homicide in Detroit 1970-1973: a test of subculture of violence theory. Diss Abs., 1975.

799. Harrison, W.R. Murder without a body--the forensic science aspect. Crim Law Rev. 1955, 158-69.

800. Hart-Hansen, J.P. Fatalities from firearms in Denmark. Forens Sci. 1974, 4, 239-245.

801. Hartman, M.S. Victorian Murderesses: A True History of Thirteen Respectable French and English Women Accused of Unspeakable Crimes. Schocken Books, N.Y. 1977.

802. Hartmann, H., Molz, G., Unexpected Death in Infancy. In: Howells, J. (ed). Modern Perspectives in the Psychiatry of Infancy. Brunner/Mazel, N.Y., 1979.

803. Hartmann, J.H. Community unemployment conditions in relation to four psycho-social indices: Mental hospitalizations, suicides, homicides, and motor vehicle accidents. Diss Abs Int. 1976, 37, 3076.

804. Hassel, C.V. The political assassin. J Pol Sci Adm. 1974, 2, 399-403.

805. Hausknecht, B.D. The "homicide scene" exception to the Fourth Amendment warrant requirement: a dead issue? J Crim Law Criminol. 1980, 3, 289-2299.

806. Havard, J.D. The legal threat to medicine. Br Med J [Clin Res]. 1982, 284, 612-3.

807. Havard, J.D. The Detection of Secret Homicide: A Study of Medico-Legal System of Investigation of Sudden and Unexplained Deaths. Macmillan, London, 1960.

808. Hawkins, D.F. Black and white homicide differentials: alternatives to an inadequate theory. Crim Just Behav. 1983, 4, 407-440.

809. Hawkins, D.F. Black homicide: the adequacy of existing research for devising prevention strategies. J Res Crime Delinq. 1985, 1, 83-103.

810. Hawkins, G. & Ward, P. Armed and disarmed police: Police firearms policy and levels of violence. J Res Crime Delinq. 1970, 7, 188-197.

811. Hawkins, D.F. Black homicide: The adequacy of existing research for devising prevention strategies. J Res Crime Delinq, 1985, 31, 83-103.

812. Hawkins, D.F. Black and white homicide differentials. Crim Just Behav. 1983, 407-40.

813. Hays, J.R., Solway, K.S. & Schreiner, D. Intellectual characteristics of juvenile murderers versus status offenders. Psychol Rep. 1978, 43, 80-2.

814. Hays, J.R., Roberts, T.K., Solway, K.S. Violence and the Violent Individual. SP Medical and Scientific, New York, 1981.

815. Hazelwood, R.R., Dietz, P.E. & Burgess, A.W. Sexual fatalities: behavioral reconstruction in equivocal cases. J Forens Sci. 1982, 27, 763-73.

816. Hazelwood, R.R. & Douglas, J.E. The lust murderer. FBI Law Enforce Bull. 1980, 1-5.

817. Healy, G.D., Aragon, K.M. & Weston, J.T. Computer support for medicolegal investigative systems. Med Law. 1983, 2, 239-47.

818. Hearne, J.G., Jr. Murder, distinction between first and second degree, inconsistency in some West Virginia cases. W Virg Law Quart. 1929, 35, 287-90.

819. Heath, A., Ahlmen, J., Branegard, B., Lindstedt, S., Wickstrom, I. & Andersen, O. Thallium poisoning--toxin elimination and therapy in three cases. J Toxicol Clin Toxicol. 1983, 20, 451-63.

820. Hedeboe, J., Charles, A.V., Nielsen, J., Grymer, F., Mller, B.N. Mller-Madsen, B. & Jensen, S.E. Interpersonal violence: patterns in a Danish community. Am J Pub Hlth. 1985, 75, 651-3.

821. Heilbrun, A.B., Jr., Heilbrun, L.C., Heilbrun, K.L. Impulsive and premediated homicide: an analysis of subsequent parole risk of the murderer. J Crim Law Criminology. 1978, 69, 108-114.

822. Heiman, M.F. The police suicide. J Pol Sci Admin. 1975, 3, 267-273.

823. Helig, S.M., Diller, J. & Nelson, F.L. A study of 44 PCP-related deaths. Int J Addict. 1982, 17, 1175-84.

824. Heller, M.S. The mentally ill offender -- the question of dangerousness. Prison J. 1969, 49, 6-12.

825. Helmholz, R.H. Infanticide in the province of Canterbury during the fifteenth century. Hist Childhood Quart. 1975, 2, 379-390.

826. Helpern, M. History of the methods of detecting murder. Am J Forens Med Pathol. 1981, 2, 61-5.

827. Helpern, M. Fatalities from child abuse and neglect: responsibility of the medical examiner and coroner. Pediatr Ann. 1976, 5, 42-57.

828. Helpern, M. Changing patterns of homicide in New York City. N.Y. State J Med. 1972, 72, 2154-7.

829. Helpern, M., Rho-Yong, M. Deaths from narcotism in New York City: incidence, circumstances, and postmortem findings. N.Y. State J Med. 1966, 66, 2391-2408.

830. Helpern, M. Postmortem examination in cases of suspected homicide. J Crim Law. 1946, 36, 485-522.

831. Helpern, M. The postmortem examination in homicides. Am J Med Jur. 1938, 1, 165-76.

832. Henderson, D.F. Settlement of homicide disputes in Sakya (Tibet). Am Anthropol. 1964, 66, 1099-1105.

833. Hendin, H. Psychotherapy for Vietnam veterans with posttraumatic stress disorders. Am J Psychother. 1983, 37, 86-99.

834. Hendrick, C., Shaffer, D.B. Murder: Effects of number of killers and victim mutilation on simulated jurors' judgments. Bull Psychon Soc. 1975, 6, 313-316.

835. Henn, F.A., Herjanic, M., Vanderpearl, R.H. Forensic psychiatry: anatomy of a service. Comp Psychiat. 1977, 18, 337-345.

836. Henn, F.A., Herjanic, M., Vanderpearl, R.H. Forensic psychiatry: diagnosis and criminal responsibility. J Nerv Ment Dis. 1976, 162, 423-429.

837. Henry, A.F. & Short, J.F. Suicide and Homicide: Some Economic Sociological, and Psychological Aspects of Aggression. Free Press, N.Y. 1954.

838. Henry, R.A. Child Homicide Victims in the United States. D.C. Heath and Company, Lexington, MA., 1980.

839. Henry, W.D. The case of Captain Colthurst. Practitioner. 1981, 225, 418-20.

840. Hentig, H.V. Some problems regarding murder detection. J Crim Law Criminol. 1938, 29, 108-118.

841. Hepburn, J. & Voss, H.L. Patterns of criminal homicide. Criminology. 1970, 8, 21-45.

842. Hepburn, J.R. Violent offenses and violent offenders. Southern Sociol Soc (SSS). 1970.

843. Herjanic, M., Henn, F.A., Vanderpearl, R.H. Forensic psychiatry: female offenders. Am J Psychiat. 1977, 134, 556-558.

844. Herjanic, M., Meyer, D.A. Psychiatric illness in homicide victims. Am J Psychiat. 1976, 133, 691-693.

845. Herjanic, M. Notes on epidemiology of homicide in an urban area. Forens Sci. 1976, 8, 235-46.

846. Hickey, J. M. Corporate criminal liability for homicide: the controversy flames anew. Cal W Law Rev. 1981, 3, 465-492.

847. Higuchi, T. & Sukegawa, Y. Statistical evaluation on cases of the forensic autopsies and the judicial examination in the southern part of Osaka City. Report of 2000 legal examinations. Osaka City Med J. 1983, 29, 185-97.

848. Hill, D. and Pond, D.A. Reflections on one hundred capital cases submitted to electroencephalography. J Ment Sci., 1952, 98, 23-43.

849. Hillard, J.R., Zung, W.W.K., Ramm, D., Holland, R.M. and Johnson, M. Accidental and homicidal death in a psychiatric emergency room population. Hosp Commun Psychiat. 1985, 36, 640-643.

850. Hilton, J.E. The duties of a police surgeon. The investigation of a sudden unexpected death and the scene of the crime. Practitioner. 1978, 221, 391-5.

851. Hingson, R., Merrigan, D. & Heeren, T. Effects of Massachusetts raising its legal drinking age from 18 to 20 on deaths from teenage homicide, suicide, and nontraffic accidents. Pediatr Clin North Am. 1985, 32, 221-32.

852. Hinton, J.W., et al. Test faking relating to a hormonal index of murderous propensity. Internat J Offend Therap Compar Criminol. 1979, 23, 257-261.

853. Hippenmeyer, R.S. Recommended change in statute defining homicide. Wisc Law Review. 1935, 10, 274-5.

854. Hirose, S. Depression and homicide. A psychiatric and forensic study of four cases. Acta Psychiatr Scand. 1979, 59, 211-7.

855. Hirsch, C.S., Rushforth, N.B., Ford, A.B., Adelson, L. Homicide and suicide in a metropolitan county. I. Long-Term trends. JAMA. 1973, 223, 900-905.

856. Hitchler, W.H. Killer and his victim in felony-murder cases. Dick Law Rev. 1948, 53, 3-11.

857. Hitcher, W.H. The new definition of murder in the first degree. 29 Dick Law Rev. 1924, 63.

858. Hobbs, A.H. Criminality in Philadelphia: 1790-1810 compared with 1937. Am Sociol Rev. 1943, 8, 198-202.

859. Hobbs, A.W. Juvenile murderers. Can Bar Rev. 1944, 22, 377-9.

860. Hoedemarker, E.D. "Irresistible impulse" as a defense in criminal law; a criticism based on modern psychiatric concepts. Wash Law Rev. 1948, 23, 1-7.

861. Hoey, L.G. Study of the phenomenological experience of the survivor-victims of homicide. Diss Abs Intern. 1984, 45, 352-353.

862. Hoffman, F.L. The increase in murder. Ann Am Acad Pol Soc Sci. 1926, 125, 20-29.

863. Hogan, B. Killing ground: 1964-73. Crim Law Rev. 1974, 1974, 387-401.

864. Hogan, H.W. Homicide patterns in New Orleans. Human Mosaic. 1969, 4, 69-80.

865. Hogan, J.C. Murder by perjury. Fordham Law Rev 1961, 30, 285.

866. Holcomb, W.R. & Adams, N. The inter-domain among personality and cognition variables in people who commit murder. J Person Assess. 1983, 47, 524-30.

867. Holcomb, W.R. & Adams, N. Racial influences on intelligence and personality measures of people who commit murder. J Clin Psychol. 1982, 38, 793-6.

868. Holcomb, W.R., Adams, N.A. & Ponder, H.M. The developmental and cross-validation of an MMPI typology of murderers. J Person Assess. 1985, 49, 240-244.

869. Holcomb, W.R., Adams, N.A. & Ponder, H.M. Are separate black and white MMPI norms needed? An IQ-controlled comparison of accused murderers. J Clin Psychol. 1984, 40, 189-93.

870. Holcomb, W.R., Adams, N.A., Ponder, H.M. & Anderson, W.P. Cognitive and behavioral predictors of MMPI scores in pretrial psychological evaluations of murderers. J Clin Psychol. 1984, 40, 592-7.

871. Holcomb, W.R. & Anderson, W.P. Alcohol and multiple drug abuse in accused murderers. Psychol Rep. 1983, 52, 159-64.

872. Holden, I.G. Homicidal poisoning. Med Sci Law. 1968, 6, 22-6.

873. Holder, A.R. Homicide by quackery. JAMA. 1972, 222, 1219-20.

874. Holinger, P.C. Self-destructiveness among the young: an epidemiological study of violent deaths. Int J Soc Psychiat. 1981, 27, 277-82.

875. Holinger, P.C. Violent deaths as a leading cause of mortality: an epidemiologic study of suicide, homicide, and accidents. Am J Psychiat. 1980, 137, 472-6.

876. Holinger, P.C. Violent deaths among the young: recent trends in suicide, homicide, and accidents. Am J Psychiat. 1979, 136, 1144-7.

877. Holinger, P.C. & Klemen, E.H. Violent deaths in the United States, 1900-1975. Relationships between suicide, homicide and accidental deaths. Soc Sci Med. 1982, 16, 1929-38.

878. Holliday, B.G. Advocacy for life: mandates, models, and priorities for prevention. Pub Hlth Rep. 1980, 95, 558-9.

879. Hollis, W.S. On the etiology of criminal homicides: The alcohol factor. J Pol Sci Adm. 1974, 2, 50-53.

880. Holme, I., Helgeland, A., Hjermann, I., Leren,P., Lund-Larsen, P.G. Four-year mortality by some socioeconomic indicator: the Oslo study. J Epidemiol Commun Hlth. 1980, 34, 48-52.

881. Homans, S.S., Curran, W.J., McGarry, A.L. Charged with murder: Six men discuss their attitudes toward trial. Mass J Ment Hlth. 1973, 3, 4-32.

882. Hooton. The American Criminal. Vol. I. Harvard Univ. Press, Cambridge, Massachusetts. 1939.

883. Horton, A.M., Johnson, C.H. The treatment of homicidal obsessional ruminations by thought-stopping and covert assertion. J Behav Ther Exper Psychiat. 1977, 8, 339-340.

884. Houk, V.W. Public health and cost implications of suicide, homicide, and criminal violence. Tex Med. 1983, 79, 6-7.

885. Houts, M. They Asked for Death. Cowles, N.Y., 1970, 241, 64-65.

886. Howard, I.J. The culpability of homicide: differential treatment towards heterosexual and homosexual perpetrators and their victims. Diss Abs Intern. 1983, 44, 2012.

887. Howell, L.M. Clinical and research impressions regarding murder and sexually perverse crimes. Psychother Psychosom. 1972-1973, 21, 156-159.

888. Hoyt, M.F. Observations regarding patients' reactions to the Jonestown massacre and the Moscone-Milk assassinations. J Am Acad Psychoanal. 1981, 9, 303-309.

889. Hudgens, R.W. Murder by a manic-depressive. Int J Neuropsychiat. 1965, 1, 381-3.

890. Hudson, P. Multishot firearm suicide. Examination of 58 cases. Am J Forensic Med pathol. 1981, 2, 239-42.

891. Hudson, R.P., Humphrey, J.A. & Kupferer, H.J. Regional variations in the characteristics of victims of violence. Int J Soc Psychiat. 1980, 26, 300-20.

892. Hudson, R.P., Humphrey, J.A., Kupferer, H.J. Regional variations in the characteristics of victims of violence. Victimology. 1977, 2, 64-65.

893. Huff, C.L., Corzine, J., & Moore, D.C. Southern exposure: Deciphering the south's influence on homicide rates. Soc Stud Soc Probl. 1985, 2408.

894. Hughes, D.J. Homicide, Investigative Techniques. C.C. Thomas, Springfield, Ill 1974.

895. Humphrey, J.A. & Palmer, S. A comparison of homicide and suicide victims in North Carolina during 1972-73. Victimology. 1977, 2, 65.

896. Humphrey, J.A. Homicide, suicide, and role relationships in New Hampshire. Diss Abs Intern. 1973, 34, 2789-2790.

897. Humphrey, J.A. & Kupferer, H.J. Homicide and suicide among the Cherokee and Lumbee Indians of North Carolina. Int J Soc Psychiat. 1982, 28, 121-8.

898. Humphrey, J.A., Kupferer, H.J. Pockets of violence: an exploration of homicide and suicide. Dis Nerv Sys. 1977, 38, 833-837.

899. Humphrey, J.A. Role interference: an analysis of suicide victims, homicide offenders, and non-violent individuals. J Clin Psychiat. 1978, 39, 652-655.

900. Humphrey, J.A. Social loss: a comparison of suicide victims, homicide offenders and non-violent individuals. Dis Nerv Sys. 1977, 38, 157-160.

901. Humphrey, J.A. Women who are murdered: An analysis of 912 consecutive victims. Omega: J Death Dying. 1981-82, 12, 281-88.

902. Humphrey, J.A., Palmer, S. Stressful life events and criminal homicide offender-victim relationships. Victimology. 1980, 5, 115-120.

903. Humphrey, J.A. & Palmer, S. Homicide and Suicide in North Carolina: An Emerging Subculture of Self-Violence? In: J.A. Inciardi, Pottieger, A.E. (eds). Violent Crime: Historical and Contemporary Issues. Sage Publications, Beverly Hills, 1980.

904. Huntington, R.W., Jr, Colt, J., Owen, F. and Younger, M. The stomped pancreas death. Amer J Surg. 1961, 102, 728-31.

905. Huntington, R.W., III and Weisberg, H.F. Unusual form of child abuse. J Forens Sci. 1977, 22, 5-6.

906. Hurnard, N.D. The King's Pardon for Homicide before A.D. 1307. Oxford Univ. Press, London, 1969.

907 . Husain, A., Anasseril, D.E., Harris, P.W. A study of young-age and mid-life homicidal women admitted to a psychiatric hospital for pre-trial evaluation. Can J Psychiat. 1983, 28, 109-113.

908 . Husain, S.A. & Daniel, A. A comparative study of filicidal and abusive mothers. Can J Psychiat. 1984, 29, 596-598.

909 . Hutzler, J.C. Family pathology in crime and punishment. Am J Psychoanal. 1979, 38, 335-42.

I

910. Irons, F., Steuterman, M.C. & Brinkhous, W. Two bite marks on assailant. Primary link to homicide conviction. Am J Forens Med Pathol. 1983, 4, 177-80.

911. Irvine, A. and Johnson, H. Murder by thallium. Med Leg J. 1974, 42, 76-90.

912. Isaacs, E.R. Modern concepts of the crime of murder: a psychopathological study. Medicoleg Bull. 1969, 189, 1-4.

913. Iserson, K.V. Strangulation: a review of ligature, manual, and postural neck compression injuries. Ann Emerg Med. 1984, 13, 179-85.

914. Iskrant, A.P. & Joliet, P.V. Accidents and Homicide. Harvard University Press, Cambridge, Massachusetts, 1968.

915. Iverson, D.C. Homicide prevention from the perspective of the Office of Health Promotion. Pub Hlth Rep. 1980, 95, 559-60.

J

916. Jackson, B. Exiles from the American Dream: The Junkie and the Cop. In: Skolnick, J. (ed). Police in America, Little, Brown, Boston, 1975, 192-203.

917. Jackson, J.D. The mens rea of murder in Northern Ireland. N Ir Legal Quart. 1981, 2, 175-187.

918. Jackson, P.G. Some effects of parole supervision on recidivism. Br J Criminol. 1983, 23, 17-34.

919. Jacobsson, L. Acts of violence in a traditional western Ethiopian society in transition. Acta Psychiatr Scand. 1985, 71, 601-7.

920. James, I.P. Necrophilia, murder and high intelligence. Br J Psychiat. 1979, 134, 125-6.

921. Janis, J.M., Deteis, R, Steele, D. & Walker, A.H. Monitoring health in Los Angeles County. Pub Hlth Rep. 1985, 100, 393-401.

922. Jansen, H. Homicidal chronic sodium chlorate poisoning. Forens Sci. 1972, 1, 103-5.

923. Jarcho, S. Malaria and murder (Joseph Jones, 1878). Bull NY Acad Med. 1968, 44, 759-60.

924. Jarvis, G.K. & Boldt, M. Death styles among Canada's Indians. Soc Sci Med. 1982, 16, 1345-52.

925. Jason, J. Centers for Disease Control and the epidemiology of violence. Child Abuse Negl. 1984, 8, 279-83.

926. Jason, J. Child homicide spectrum. Am J Dis Child. 1983, 137, 578-81.

927 . Jones, A.M. & Chapman, A.J. Intramural ventricular fibroma of the heart. Incidental finding in a homicide victim. Am J Forens Med Pathol. 1983, 4, 73-7.

928 . Jones, H. Crime in Guyana. Some problems of comparative study in the Caribbean. Soc Econ Stud. 1980, 20, 60-68.

929 . Jones, J. Unusual blood evidence in a homicide a century ago. Am J Forens Med Pathol. 1982, 3, 231-239.

930 . Jonsson, J. & Voigt, G.E. Homicidal intoxications by lye - and parachlorcresol-containing disinfectants. Am J Forens Med Pathol. 1984, 5, 57-63.

931 . Juve, J.L. Bad drug trips and flashbacks. Child Welfare. 1972, 52, 41-50.

K

932. Kahn, M.W., Raifman, L. Hospitalization versus imprisonment and the insanity plea. Crim Just Behav. 1981, 8, 483-490.

933. Kahn, M.W. Murderers who plead insanity: A descriptive factor-analytic study of personality, social, and history variables. Genet Psychol Monographs. 1971, 84, 275-360.

934. Kahn, M.W. Correlates of Rorschach reality adherence in the assessment of murderers who plead insanity. J Project Tech Person Assess. 1967, 31, 44-47.

935. Kahn, M.W. Psychological test study of a mass murderer. J Project Tech Person Assess. 1960, 24, 148-60.

936. Kakar, S. Aggression in Indian society: An analysis of folk-tales. Ind J Psychol. 1974, 49, 119-126.

937. Kaliappan, K.V. & Shanmugam, T.E. Somatic defense and anxiety reduction: A preliminary report. Ind J Appl Psychol. 1982, 19, 34-36.

938. Kalisch, B.J., Kalisch, P.A. & Livesay, E. When nurses are accused of murder: the melodramatic effects of media coverage. Nurs Life. 1982, 2, 44-7.

939. Kalisch, P.A., Kalisch, B.J. & Livesay, E. The "Angel of Death": the anatomy of 1980's major news story about nursing. Nurs Forum. 1980, 19, 212-41.

940. Kania, R.R.E. & Mackey, W.C. Police violence as a function of community characteristics. Criminology. 1977, 15, 27-48.

941 . Kaplun, D. & Reich, R. The murdered child and his killers. Am J Psychiat. 1976, 133, 809-813.

942 . Kaplun, D., Reich, R. The murdered child and his killers. Ann Prog Child Psychiat Child Develop. 1977, 652-661.

943 . Kappel, W.W. A biological face: Violent deaths in an antiviolent town's record of a century of life and death. Aggress Behav. 1979, 5, 213-214.

944 . Karazulas, C.P. The presentation of bite mark evidence resulting in the acquittal of a man after serving seven years in prison for murder. J Forens Sci. 1984, 29, 355-8.

945 . Karpman, B. The Sexual Offender and His Offenses. Julian Press, N.Y., 1954.

946 . Karpman, B. Psychoanalytic study of a case of murder. Psychoanal Rev. 1951, 38, 245-270.

947 . Kates, D.B., Jr. Reflections on the relevancy of gun control. Crim Law Bull. 1977, 13, 119-124.

948 . Katsumata, Y., Ito, H., Sato, K., Sato, M. & Yada, S. A case of strangulation with postmortem amputation of the penis. J Forens Sci. 1984, 29, 934-7.

949 . Katz, M.L. A comparison of ego functioning in filicidal and physically child-abusing mothers. Diss Abs Intern. 1976, 36, 5798.

950 . Kazamatsuri, H., Nanko, S. & Mato, Y. Homicidality in a woman with a 47,xxx karyotype. J Clin Psychiatry. 1985, 46, 346-7.

951 . Keedy, E.R. History of the Pennsylvania statute creating degrees of murder. Univ Penn Law Rev. 1951, 39, 469-71.

952 . Keedy, E.R. Problem of first degree murder: Fisher v. United States. Univ Penn Law Rev. 1950, 99, 267-92.

953 . Kellerman, J. Hypnosis as an adjunct to thought-stopping and covert reinforcement in the treatment of homicidal obsessions in a twelve-year-old boy. Int J Clin Exp Hypn. 1981, 29, 128-35.

954 . Kelly, H.E. A comparison of defense strategy and race as influences in differential sentencing. Criminology. 1976, 14, 241-249.

955. Kendall, R.E. Relationship between aggression and depression epidemiological implications of a hypothesis. Arch Gen Psychiat. 1970, 22, 308-318.

956. Kenney, J.P. Forensic dentistry: from denture identification to murder investigations. Dent Assist. 1982, 51, 17-20.

957. Kenny, P.H. Making homicides pay? J Crim Law. 1983, 4, 271-275.

958. Kenyon, F.E. Emergencies in child psychiatry. J Ment Sci Law. 1961, 1616.

959. Kermani, E.J. Violent psychiatric patients: A study. Am J Psychotherapy. 1981, 35, 215-225.

960. Ketner, L.G., Humphrey, J.A. Homicide, sex role differences and role relationships. J Death Dying. 1979-80, 10, 379-86.

961. Kiel, F.W. The psychiatric character of the assailant as determined by autopsy observations of the victim. J Forens Sci. 1965, 19, 263-71.

962. Kim, Y.S. Mortality of the Korean population in Japan: a life table analysis of selected causes of death. J Biosoc Sci. 1982, 14, 465-72.

963. King, C.H. Counter-transference and counter-experience in the treatment of violence prone youth. Am J Orthopsychiat. 1976, 46, 43-52.

964. King, C.H. The ego and the integration of violence in homicidal youth. Am J Orthopsychiat. 1975, 45, 134-45.

965. King, D.R. The brutalization effect: execution publicity and the incidence of homicide in South Carolina. Soc Forces. 1978, 57, 683-687.

966. King, L.A. & Jobson, D. An unusual carbon monoxide poisoning involving a caravan. J Forens Sci Soc. 1982, 22, 137-9.

967. King, L.J. Alcohol abuse: A crucial factor in the social problems of negro men. Am J Psychiat. 1969, 125, 1682-1690.

968. King, L.J. Alcoholism: Studies Regarding Black Americans, 1977-1980. In: T.D. Watts (ed). Black Alcoholism: Toward a Comprehensive Understanding. C.C. Thomas, Springfield, Ill. 1981.

969. Kippax, D.E. The lust murder of Edward. Aust NZ J Psychiat. 1982, 16, 161-8.

970. Kiremidjian, D. Crime and punishment; Matricide and the woman question. Am Imago. 1976, 33, 403-433.

971. Kirk, A.R. Black Homicide. In: B.L. Danto (ed). The Human Side of Homicide. Columbia Univ Press, N.Y., 1982, 138-155.

972. Kirkpatrick, J.T. The lives of criminally violent women: I and II. Diss Abs Intern. 1984, 45, 652.

973. Kirwan, W.E. Mistakes in homicide investigation. Med Trial Tech Quart. 1966, 12, 23-43.

974. Kivela, S.L. Relationship between suicide, homicide and accidental deaths among the aged in Finland in 1951-1979. Acta Psychiat Scand. 1985, 155-160.

975. Kjervik, D.K. The psychiatric nurse's duty to warn potential victims of homicidal psychotherapy outpatients. Law Med Hlth Care. 1981, 9, 11-6.

976. Klamt, R.R. Homicide and LSD. JAMA. 1973, 224, 246.

977. Klebba, A.J. Homicide trends in the United States, 1900-74. Pub Hlth Rep. 1975, 90, 195-204.

978. Kleck, G. Capital punishment, gun ownership, and homicide. Am J Sociol. 1979, 84, 882-910.

979. Kleck, G. Racial discrimination in criminal sentencing; A critical evaluation of the evidence with additional evidence on the death penalty. Am Sociol Rev. 1981, 46, 783-805.

980. Klein, D., Reizen, M.S. Van-Amburg, G.H., Walker, S.A. Some social characteristics of young gunshot fatalities. Accid Anal Prevent. 1977, 9, 177-182.

981. Klepfiaz, A. & Racy, J. Homicide and LSD. JAMA. 1973, 223, 429-430.

982. Klerman, G.L. Homicide among black males. Pub Hlth Rep. 1980, 95, 561.

983. Kline, M.V. Defending the mentally ill: the insanity defense and the role of forensic hypnosis. Int J Clin Exp Hypn. 1979, 27, 375-401.

984 . Klinger, B.I. Replication in studies of the insanity plea. Am J Psychiat. 1980, 137, 133.

985 . Knight, B. Ricin--a potent homicidal poison. Br Med J. 1979, 1, 350-1.

986 . Knudson, K. Homicide after treatment with lysergic acid diethylamide. Acta Scand Psychiat Supp. 40, 180.

987 . Knudten, R.D. Criminal Violations Against the Person. In: Knudten, R. (ed). Crime in a Complex Society. Dorsey Press, Homewood, Ill., 1970, 119-154.

988 . Kobbervig, W., Inverarity, J. & Lauderdale, P. Deterrence and the death penalty: A comment on Phillips. Am J Sociol. 1982, 88, 1, 161-164.

989 . Kobler, A.L. Police homicide in a democracy. J Soc Iss. 1975, 31, 163-184.

990 . Kobler, A.L. Figures (and perhaps some facts) on police killing of civilians in the United States, 1965-1969. J Soc Iss. 1975, 31, 185-191.

991 . Koenig, D.M. Capital punishment and crimes of murder. Loy Law J. 1982, 4, 817-840.

992 . Koranda, H. Cooling time, a desirable test. J Crim Law. 1939, 30, 130-2.

993 . Kothe, K. From behavioral psychology -- case of a young murderer after his deed. Psychiat Neurol. 1963, 146, 16-28.

994 . Kozma, C. & Zuckerman, M. An investigation of some hypotheses concerning rape and murder. Personal Indiv Diff. 1983, 4, 23-29.

995 . Kozma, C.L. An investigation of some hypotheses concerning rape and murder. Diss Abs Intern. 1978, 39, 1485.

996 . Kraus, J. Trends in violent crime and public concern. Aust J Soc Iss. 1979, 14, 175-191.

997 . Krauss, T.C. & Warlen, S.C. The forensic science use of reflective ultraviolet photography. J Forens Sci. 1985, 30, 262-8.

998 . Kressel, G.M. Sororicide-filiacide-homicide for family honour. Curr Anthropol. 1981, 22, 141, 158.

999 . Krevat, M.E. Evidence of homicide victim's prior acts of misconduct admissible in self-defense claim. Suffolk Univ Law Rev. 1982, 2, 567-573.

1000 . Kringsholm, B., Voigt, J., Dalgaard, J.B. & Simonsen, J. Deaths among narcotic addicts in Denmark in 1978 and 1979. Forens Sci Int. 1981, 18, 19-30.

1001 . Krishna, K.P. Murdered and the murderer. Ind J Soc Work. 1982, 43, 83-90.

1002 . Krishna, K.P. Suicide and homicide in India. Ind J Criminol Criminalistics. 1981, 1, 107-108.

1003 . Krohn, M.D. Inequality, unemployment and crime: a cross-national analysis. Soc Quart. 1976, 17, 303-313.

1004 . Krohn, M.D. A Durkheimian analysis of international crime rates. Soc Forces. 1978, 57, 654-670.

1005 . Kroll, J. & Mackenzie, T.B. When psychiatrists are liable: risk management and violent patients. Hosp Commun Psychiat. 1983, 34, 29-36.

1006 . Kroll, P., et al. Denying the incredible: unexplained deaths in a Veterans Administration hospital. Am J Psychiat. 1977, 134, 1376-80.

1007 . Kromm, J., Vasile, R.G. & Gutheil, T.G. Occupational therapy in the assessment of a woman accused of murder. Psychiatr Quart. 1982, 54, 85-96.

1008 . Kruckenberg, J.M. Characteristics of homicide and its prevention. Diss Abs Intern. 1978, 38, 5576.

1009 . Krupp, R.C. A profile and analysis of convicted murderers. Diss Abs Intern. 1984, 44, 2589-2590.

1010 . Krystal, H. The Psychoanalytic (Self-Conscious) Approach to Aggression: Affect and Act. In: B. Danto, J. Bruhns & A.H. Kutscher (eds). The Human Side of Homicide, Columbia Univ Press, N.Y., 1982, 50-72.

1011 . Kua, E.H., Ang, A.L. & Yuan, A.F. Homicide and mental illness in Singapore. Singa Med J. 1984, 25, 61-3.

1012. Kua, E.H., Yuan, A.F. & Ang, A.L. Homicide in Singapore. Med Sci Law. 1985, 25, 26-8.

1013. Kundu, R., Bhaumik, G. Some affective personality qualities of murderer: A research note. Personal Stud Group Behav. 1982, 2, 36-43.

1014. Kunitz, S.J. & Edland, J.F. The epidemiology of autopsies in Monroe County, N.Y. J Forens Sci. 1973, 18, 370-379.

1015. Kunkle, S. & Humphrey, J.A. Murder of the elderly: An analysis of increased vulnerability. Omega. 1982-83, 13, 27-34.

1016. Kunz, P.R. & Summers, J. A time to die: A study of the relationship of birthdays and time of death. Omega. 1980, 10, 281-289.

1017. Kuo, M.C. Linking a bloodstain to a missing person by genetic inheritance. J Forens Sci. 1982, 27, 438-44.

1018. Kupferer, H.J. & Humphrey, J.A. Fatal Indian violence in North Carolina. Anthropol Quart. 1975, 48, 236, 244.

1019. Kurland, A.A., Morgenstern, J. and Sheets, C. A comparative study of wife murderers admitted to a State Psychiat Therapy. 1955, 1, 7-15.

L

1020. Lachman, E. Physician, educator, anatomist and mass murderer. J Okla State Med Assoc. 1978, 71, 354-7.

1021. Lachman, J.H. & Cravens, J.M. The murderers-before and after. Psychiatr Quart. 1969, 43, 1-11.

1022. Lagner, H.P. The making of a murderer. Am J Psychiat. 1971, 127, 950-3.

1023. Lalli, M. & Turner, S.H. Suicide and homicide: A comparative analysis by race and occupational levels. J Crim Law Criminol. 1968, 59, 191-200.

1024. Lancaster, N.P. Necrophilia, murder and high intelligence: A case report. Brit J Psychiat. 1978, 132, 605-608.

1025. Landau, S.F. Pathologies among homicide offenders: Some cultural profiles. Br J Criminol. 1975, 15, 157-166.

1026. Landau, S.F., Drapkin, I., Arad, S. Homicide victims and offenders: An Israeli study. J Crim Law Criminol. 1974, 65, 390-396.

1027. Landau, S.F. Type of Homicide and Pathologies Among Homicide Offenders: Some Cultural Profiles. In: M. Riedel & T.P. Thornberry (eds.) Crime and Delinquency: Dimensions of Deviance. Praeger, N.Y., 1974, 211.

1028. Lander, J. Homicide acting out and impulse. Amer J Orthopsychiat. 1963, 33, 928-30.

1029. Landy, D. & Aronson, E. The influence of the character of the criminal and his victim on the decisions of simulated jurors. J Exper Soc Psychol. 1969, 5, 141-152.

1030. Lane, R.C. Robert Lindner and the case of Charles: A teenage sex murderer: "Songs my mother taught me". Curr Iss Psychoanal Pract. 1984, 1, 65-83.

1031. Langevin, R., Paitich, D., Orchard, B., Handy, L. & Russon, A. Childhood and family background of killers seen for psychiatric assessment: a controlled study. Bull Am Acad Psychiat Law. 1983, 11, 331-41.

1032. Langevin, R., Paitich, D., Orchard, B., Handy, L., & Russon, A. The role of alcohol, drugs, suicide attempts and situational strains in homicide committed by offenders seen for psychiatric assessment. A controlled study. Acta Psychiatr Scand. 1982, 66, 229-42.

1033. Langevin, R., Paitich, D., Orchard, B., Handy, L. & Russon, A. Diagnosis of killers seen for psychiatric assessment. A controlled study. Acta Psychiatr Scand. 1982, 66, 216-28.

1034. Langslow, A. "Most heinous of crimes". Part II. Aust Nurses J. 1984, 14, 65-6, 69.

1035. Langslow, A. Nurse & the law. Most heinous of crimes, 1. Aust Nurses J. 1984, 14, 55-6.

1036. Langslow, A. The nurse and the law. High drama lay in nursing notes. Aust Nurses J. 1984, 13, 33-5, 52.

1037. Lanzkron, J. Murder and insanity: a survey. Am J Psychiat. 1963, 119, 754-8.

1038. Lapham, S.C., Weber, S.F., Burkhart, M.J., Hoffman, R.E. & Kreiss, K. Risk factors for victimization during the 1980 riot at the Penitentiary of New Mexico. Am J Epidemiol. 1984, 119, 218-26.

1039. Lasaga, J.I. Death in Jonestown: Techniques of political control by a paranoid leader. Suicide Life Threat Behav. 1980, 10, 210-213.

1040. Latham, J.A., Jr. Torts -- Duty to act for protection of another -- Liability of psychotherapist for failure to warn of homicide threatened by patient. Vanderbilt Law Rev. 1975, 28, 631-640.

1041. Laufer, W.S., Johnson, J.A., Hogan, R. Ego control and criminal behavior. J Personal Soc Psychol. 1981, 41, 179-184.

1042. Lawrence, C.E., Reilly, A.A., Quickenton, P., Greenwald, P., Page, W.F. & Kuntz, A.J. Mortality patterns of New York State Vietnam Veterans. Am J Pub Hlth. 1985, 75, 277-9.

1043. Lawton, E.G. Persons who injure others: A study of criminally assaultive behaviour in Philadelphia. (1975). Diss Abs Intern. 1979, 40, 3549-A.

1044. LeBlang, T.R. Hypnosis of witness becomes focus of murder defense. Leg Aspects Med Pract. 1979, 7, 31-3.

1045. LeBlond, S. The anatomists and the resurrectionists in Great Britain. II. Murder for anatomy. Can Med Assoc. 1965, 93, 113-20.

1046. Lee, A.S. & Lee, E.S. The health of slaves and the health of freedmen: A Savannah study. Phylon. 1977, 38, 170-180.

1047. Leffers, B. & Jeanty, D. Handgun pellet ammunition ("snake shot") wounds: report of three cases. J Forens Sci. 1982, 27, 433-7.

1048. Lefkowitz, B. and Gross, K.G. Victims: The Wylie-Hoffert Murder Case and its Strange Aftermath. G. Putnam & Sons, N.Y., 1969.

1049. Lehmann, N. Alcohol-related domestic violence: Clinical implications and intervention strategies. Alcohol Treat Quart. 1984, 1, 111-115.

1050. Lehrman, N.S. The Berwid case. N.Y. State J Med. 1985, 85, 198-9.

1051. Lehtinen, M.W. The value of life: An argument for the death penalty. J Crime Delinq. 1977, 23, 237-252.

1052. Leibman, J.H. Reckless homicide. Am Bus Law J. 1981, 4, 588-591.

1053. Leiden, C. Assassination in the Middle East. Transaction. 1969, 6, 20-23.

1054. Leiman, S.Z. Therapeutic homicide: a philosophic and Halakhic critique of Harris' 'survival lottery'. J Med Philos. 1983, 8, 257-67.

1055 . Lempert, R. The effect of executions on homicides: a new look in an old light. J Crime Delinq. 1983, 1, 88-115.

1056 . Lerner, M. & Nurco, D.N. Drug abuse deaths in Baltimore, 1951-1966. Int J Addict. 1970, 5, 693-716.

1057 . LeRouax L.C., Smith, L.S. Violent deaths and alcoholic intoxication. J Forens Med. 1964, 11, 131-147.

1058 . Lesse, S. The psychiatrist in court--theatre of the absurd. Am J Psychother. 1982, 36, 287-91.

1059 . Lester, D Conformity, suicide and homicide. Behav Sci Res. 1982, 17, 24-30.

1060 . Lester, D. The prevention of homicide. Crisis Intervent. 1972, 4, 105-111.

1061 . Lester, D., Perdue, W.C. Body image of murderers. J Gen Psychol. 1974, 90, 187-189.

1062 . Lester, D., Perdue, W.C., Brookhart, D. Murder and the control of aggression. Psychol Rep. 1974, 34, 706.

1063 . Lester, D., Perdue, W.C., Brookhart, D. Murderers who have attempted suicide. Psychol Rep. 1974, 35, 238.

1064 . Lester, D. A cross-national study of suicide and homicide. Behav Sci Res. 1974, 9, 307-318.

1065 . Lester, D., Kendra, J.M., Perdue, W.C. Distinguishing murderers from suicides with Rorschach. Percept Mot Skills. 1974, 39, 474.

1066 . Lester, D. Ellen West's suicide as a case of psychic homicide. Psychoanal Rev. 1971, 58, 251-263.

1067 . Lester, D. External restraints, suicide and homicide: Comparison of Norway and France. Percept Motor Skills. 1973, 36, 646.

1068 . Lester, D. The prediction of suicide and homicide rates cross-nationally by means of stepwise multiple regression. Behav Sci Res. 1977, 12, 61-69.

1069. Lester, D. Freedom of the press and personal violence: A cross-national study of suicide and homicide. J Soc Psychol. 1981, 114, 267-269.

1070. Lester, D., Homicides and the death penalty. JAMA. 1973, 225, 313.

1071. Lester, D. Internal conflict and personal violence: A cross-national study of suicide and homicide. Int J Group Tensions. 1978, 8, 68-70.

1072. Lester, D. Mortality rates and aggression management. Psychol Rep. 1973, 33, 865-866.

1073. Lester, D. Murder: A review. Correct Soc Psychiat J Appl Behav Ther. 1973, 19, 40-50.

1074. Lester, D. National homicide and suicide rates as a function of political stability. Psychol Rep. 1973, 33, 298.

1075. Lester, D. National motives and psychogenic death rates. Science. 1968, 161, 1260.

1076. Lester, D., Kendra, J.M. Thisted, R.A. Prediction of homicide and suicide: a test in a healthy risk-taking group. Percept Mot Skills. 1977, 44, 222.

1077. Lester, D. Prediction of homicide with the Rorschach. J Clin Psychol. 1975, 31, 752.

1078. Lester, D. Regional variation in suicide and homicide. J Suicide Life Threat Behav. 1985, 15, 110-6.

1079. Lester, D. Sex differences in the homicide rate. Psychol Rep. 1973, 33, 250.

1080. Lester, D. Status integration and homicide. Psychol Rep. 1973, 32, 774.

1081. Lester, D. Suicide and homicide: Bias in the examination of the relationship between suicide and homicide rates. Soc Psychiat. 1971, 6, 80-82.

1082. Lester, D. Suicide and homicide in open and closed societies. Psychol Rep. 1971, 29, 430.

1083. Lester, D. Suicide, homicide, and age dependency ratios. Aging Hum Develop. 1973, 4, 127-132.

1084. Lester, D., Perdue, W.C. Suicide, homicide and color-shading on the Rorschach. Percept Mot Skills. 1972, 35, 562.

1085 . Lester, D. The association between the quality of life and suicide and homicide rates. J Soc Psychol. 1984, 124, 247-8.

1086 . Lester, D., Murrell, M.E. The preventive effect of strict gun control laws on suicide and homicide. J Suicide Life Threat Behav. 1982, 12, 131-40.

1087 . Lester, D. Variation in homicide rate with latitude and longitude in the United States. Percept Mot Skills. 1973, 36, 532.

1088 . Lester, D. Variation in suicide and homicide rates by latitude and longitude in the United States, Canada, and Australia. Am J Psychiat. 1985, 142, 523-4.

1089 . Lester, D. Variation in suicide and homicide by latitude and longitude. Percept Motor Skills. 1980, 51, 1346.

1090 . Lester, D. Handgun control laws, suicide, and homicide. Am J Psychiat. 1985, 142, 144.

1091 . Lester, D. Suicide and homicide in U.S. prisons. Am J Psychiat. 1982, 139, 1527-8.

1092 . Lester, D. Police officers killed and the guns used by criminals. Psychol Rep. 1982, 50, 1206.

1093 . Lester, D. Alcohol and suicide and homicide. J Stud Alc. 1980, 41, 1220-3.

1094 . Lester, D. Effect of Gary Gilmore's execution on homicidal behavior. Psychol Rep. 1980, 47, 1262.

1095 . Lester, D. Deterring effect of executions on murder as a function of number and proportion of executions. Psychol Rep. 1979, 45, 598.

1096 . Lester, D. Executions as a deterrent to homicides. Psychol Rep. 1979, 44, 562.

1097 . Lester, D. Temporal variation in suicide and homicide. Am J Epidemiol. 1979, 109, 517-20.

1098 . Lester, D. & Murrell, M.E. The preventive effect of strict gun control laws on suicide and homicide. J Suicide Life Threat Behav. 1982, 12, 131-40.

1099 . Lester, D. The relationship between suicide and homicide. Correct Soc Psychiat. 1977, 23, 83-84.

1100 . Lester, D. & Wright, T. Murderers and overcontrolled hostility. Psychol Rep. 1978, 43, 1202.

1101 . Lester, D. Homicidal and suicidal impulses in the Nazi leaders. Percept Mot Skills. 1976, 43, 1316.

1102 . Lester, D. Suicide, homicide, and the effects of socialization. J Person Soc Psychol. 1967, 5, 466-468.

1103 . Lester, D. The murder of police officers in American cities. Crim Just Behav. 1984, 11, 101-113.

1104 . Lester, D., Lester, G. Crime of Passion: Murder and the Murderer. Nelson-Hall, Chicago, 1975.

1105 . Lester, D. Suicide and homicide rates and the society's need for affiliation. J Cross-Cult Psychol. 1971, 2, 405-406.

1106 . Lester, D. A study of civilian-caused murders of police officers. Int J Crim Penol. 1978, 6, 373-378.

1107 . Lester, D. Corn consumption, tryptophan and cross-national homicide and suicide rates. J Orthomol Psychiat. 1985, 14, 178-179.

1108 . Lester, D. The detection of attempted suicides and murderers using the Rorschach. J Psychiatr Res. 1974, 10, 101-3.

1109 . Levi, K. Homicide and suicide: Structure and process. Deviant Behav. 1982, 3, 91-115.

1110 . Levi, K. Homicide as conflict resolution. Deviant Behav. 1980, 1, 281-308.

1111 . Levie, R.C. A study of criminal homicide patterns and selected characteristics of victims and offenders in the city of New Orleans, 1971-73. Diss Abs Intern. 1979, 40, 3071.

1112. Levin, M.S. Drunk driving homicide - murder or enhanced manslaughter? Calif Law Rev. 1983, 4, 1298-1323.

1113. Levine, L.J. Forensic dentistry: our most controversial case. Leg Med Annu. 1978, 73-101.

1114 . Levine, L.J. The solution of a battered-child homicide by dental evidence: report of case. J Am Dent Assoc. 1973, 87, 1234-6.

1115 . Levy, J.E., Kunitz, S.J. & Everett, M. Navajo criminal homicide. Southwest J Anthropol. 1969, 25, 124-152.

1116 . Lewin, B.D. Child psychiatry in the 1830's--Three little homicidal monomaniacs. Psychoanal Stud Child. 1949, 3, 489-493.

1117 . Lewin, T. The family secret: The case of the 29-year-old murders. Nat Law J. 1981, 8.

1118 . Lewis, C.E., Cloninger, C.R. and Pais, J. Alcoholism, antisocial personality and drug use in a criminal population. Alc Alcohol. 1983, 18, 53-60.

1119 . Lewis, C.N. Memory adaptation to psychological trauma. Am J Psychoanal. 1980, 40, 419-323.

1120 . Lewis, C.N. & Arsenian, J. Murder will out: A case of parricide in a painter and his painting. J Nerv Ment Dis. 1977, 164, 273-279.

1121 . Lewis, C.N. & Arsenian, J. Psychological resolution of homicide after 10 years. J Person Assess. 1982, 46, 647-57.

1122 . Lewis, D.O., Moy, E., Jackson, L.D., Aaronson, R., Restifo, N., Serra, S. & Simos, A. Biopsychosocial characteristics of children who later murder: a prospective study. Am J Psychiat. 1985, 142, 1161-7.

1123 . Lewis, D.O., Shanok, S.S., Grant, M. & Ritvo, E. Homicidally aggressive young children: neuropsychiatric and experimental correlates. Am J Psychiat. 1983, 140, 148-53.

1124. Lidberg, Law, Tuck, J.R., Asberg, M., Scalia-Tomba, G.P., Bertilsson, L. Homicide, suicide and CSF 5-HIAA. Acta Psychiatr Scand. 1985, 71, 230-6.

1125. Lieber, A.L., Sherin, C.R. Homicides and the lunar cycle: toward a theory of lunar influence on human emotional disturbance. Am J Psychiat. 1972, L29, 69-74.

1126. Lieber, A.L. Human aggression and the lunar synodic cycle. J Clin Psychiat. 1978, 39, 385-397.

1127. Lifton, R.J. Medicalized killing in Auschwitz. Psychiatry. 1982, 45, 283-97.

1128. Light, S.C. Multicollinearity in a study of regional variations in homicide rates: A comment on Smith and Parker. Soc Forces. 1984, 72, 800-803.

1129. Lindauer, H.D. Evidence in mitigation or excuse after proof of homicide. J Crim Law. 1935, 26, 617-18.

1130. Lindqvist, P. Criminal homicide in northern Sweden 1970-1981 - alcohol-intoxication, alcohol-abuse and mental disease. Intern J Law Psychiat. 1986, 8, 19-37.

1131. Lion, J.R. Clinical and social aspects of violence. Trans Stud Coll Physic Phila. 1982, 4, 59-73.

1132. Livingston, S. Epilepsy and murder. JAMA. 1964, 188, 13.

1133. Ljunggren, B., et al. The good old method of the nail. Surg Neurol. 1977, 7, 288-92.

1134. Lloyd, J.B. Gas chromatographic characterization of cooking fats with reference to a case of murder. J Chromatogr. 1973, 77, 228-32.

1135. Lo, B. The death of Clarence Herbert: withdrawing care is not murder. Ann Intern Med. 1984, 101, 248-51.

1136. Lobinger, C.S. Homicide concept--A study in comparative criminal law. J Crim Law Criminol. 1918, 9, 373-377.

1137. Loftin, C. & Hill, R.H. Regional subculture and homicide: An examination of the Gastil-Hackney thesis. Am Sociol Rev. 1974, 39, 714-724.

1138. Loftin, C. & McDowall, D. "One with a gun gets you two": Mandatory sentencing and firearms violence in Detroit. Ann Am Acad Polit Soc Sci. 1981, 455, 150-167.

1139. Logan, C.H. Arrest rates and deterrence. Soc Sci Quart. 1975, 56, 376-389.

1140. Lombroso. Crime, its Causes and Remedies. Little, Brown and Co., Boston. 1911.

1141. London, L.S. Psychopathologic aspects of murder. J Crim Psychopath. 1944, 5, 795-812.

1142. Lovitt, C.R. Murder in the first person: Strategy in murderers' narratives. Diss Abs Intern. 1982, 43, 164.

1143. Lowe, J.T. Murder and the reasonable man. Crim Law Rev. 1958, 1958, 453.

1144. Luchins, D.J., Sherwood, P.M., Gillin, J.C., Mendelson, W.B., Wyatt, R.J. Filicide during psychotropic-induced somnambulism: a case report. Am J Psychiat. 1978, 135, 1404-5.

1145. Luckenbill, D.F. Murder and Assault. In: R.F. Meier (ed.) Major Forms of Crime. Sage Publications, Beverly Hills, 1984, 19-45.

1146. Luckenbill, D.F. Criminal homicide as a situated transaction. Soc Prob. 1977, 25, 176-186.

1147. Luke, J.L. Recovery of intact respiratory epithelium from a cloth pillowcase four days following its utilization as a smothering instrument. J Forens Sci. 1969, 14, 389-401.

1148. Luke, J.L. Strangulation as a method of homicide. Study 1965-1966 in New York City. Arch Path. 1967, 83, 64-70.

1149. Luke, J.L. Pediatric forensic pathology. I Death by homicide. J Forens Sci. 1967, 12, 421-30.

1150. Lunde, D.T. Murder and Madness. San Francisco Book Company, San Francisco, 1976.

1151. Lunden, W.A. Violent crimes in Japan in war and peace, 1933-74. Intern J Criminol Penol. 1976, 4, 349-363.

1152. Lundsgaarde, H.P. Cultural Sanctions of Urban Homicide. In: Rose, H.M. (ed) Lethal Aspects of Urban Violence. Lexington Books, Lexington, MA., 1979, 69-90.

1153. Lundsgaarde, H.P. Murder in Space City: A Cultural Analysis of Houston Homicide Patterns. Oxford Univ Press, N.Y., 1977.

1154. Luntz, L.L. A case in forensic odontology: a bite-mark in a multiple homicide. Oral Surg. 1973, 30, 72-8.

1155. Lustgarten, E. The Fatal Chance; Twelve Cases from the Notebook of a Crime Pathologist. Peter Davies, London, 1969.

1156. Lustgarten, E. Business of Murder. C. Scribners, N.Y., 1968.

1157. Lynch, B.E. Detection of deception: Its application to forensic psychiatry. Bull Am Acad Psychiat Law. 1979, 7, 239-44.

1158. Lynch, P.P. No Remedy for Death; Memoirs of a Pathologist. Longman`s, London, 1970.

1159. Lynch, R. Comments on "homicides and the lunar cycle." Am J Psychiat 1974, 131, 230.

1160. Lyons, H. Depressive illness and aggression in Belfast. Br Med J. 1972, 1, 342-344.

1161. Lyster, W.R. Homicide and fertility rates in the United States. Soc Biol. 1974, 21, 389-392.

M

1162. Maakestad, W.J. A historical survey of corporate homicide in the United States: Could not be prosecuted in Illinois? Ill Bar J. 1981, 12, 772-779.

1163. MacCulloch, M.J., Snowden, P.R., Wood, P.J. & Mills, H.E. Sadistic fantasy, sadistic behaviour and offending. Br J Psychiat. 1983, 143, 20-9.

1164. MacDonald, J.M. Psychiatry and the Criminal: A Guide to Psychiatric Examinations for the Criminal Courts. C.C. Thomas, Springfield, Ill.,1976.

1165. MacDonald, J.M. Homicidal Threats. C.C. Thomas, Springfield, Ill. 1968.

1166. MacDonald, J.M. Homicidal threats. Am J Psychiat. 1967, 124, 475-482.

1167. MacDonald, J.M. The Murderer and His Victim. C.C. Thomas, Springfield, Ill. 1961.

1168. MacDonald, J.M. Suicide and homicide by automobile. Am J Psychiat. 1964, 121, 366-70.

1169. MacDonald, J.M. The threat to kill. Am J Psychiat. 1963, 120, 125-30.

1170. MacKinnon, P. Euthanasia and homicide. Crim Law Quart. 1984, 4, 483-508.

1171. Macleod, C.M.: A "Ripper" handwriting analysis. Criminologist. 1978-1979, 3, 120.

1172. Macleod, R.J. A child is charged with homicide: his family responds. Br J Psychiat. 1982, 141, 199-201.

1173 . Macpherson, R.K. A case of manslaughter by heat-stroke. Med J Aust. 1976, 2, 929-36.

1174 . Malmquist, C.P. & Meehl, P.E. Barabbas: a study in guilt-ridden homicide. Intern Rev Psychoanal. 1978, 5, 149-174.

1175 . Malmquist, C.P. Premonitory signs of homicidal aggression in juveniles. Am J Psychiat. 1971, 128, 461-465.

1176 . Malmquist, C.P. Psychiatric aspects of familicide. Bull Am Acad Psychiat Law. 1980, 8, 298-304.

1177 . Maltby, J.R. Criminal use of anaesthetic drugs. Anaesthesia. 1977, 32, 212-3.

1178 . Maltby, J.R. Criminal poisoning with anaesthetic drugs: murder, manslaughter, or not guilty. J Forens Sci. 1975, 6, 91-108.

1179 . Mandal, A.K., Thadepalli, H., Matory, E., Lou, M.A., & O'Donnell, V.A. Jr. Evaluation of antibiotic therapy and surgical techniques in cases of homicidal wounds of the colon. Am Surg. 1984, 50, 254-7.

1180 . Maney, A.C., Kedem, B. A binary time-series analysis of domestic child homicide: On monitoring critical, rare criteria of system performance. Evaluat Rev. 1982, 6, 393-402.

1181 . Mann, A. Homicide -- Is it objective or subjective? (Subjective view). Ky Law J. 1947, 35, 252-6.

1182 . Mant, A.K. Genocide. J Forens Sci Soc. 1978, 18, 13-7.

1183 . Mark, V.H. & Ervin, F.R. Violence and the Brain. Harper and Row, N.Y., 1970.

1184 . Marohn, R.C., Locke, E.M., Rosenthal, R. & Curtiss, G. Juvenile delinquents and violent death. Adolesc Psychiat. 1982, 10, 147-70.

1185 . Marshburn, J.H. Murder and Witchcraft in England, 1550-1640: As Recounted in Pamphlets, Ballads, Broadsides, and Plays. Univ Oklahoma Press, Norman, Oklahoma, 1972.

1186 . Marten, M.E. The Doctor Looks at Murder. Doubleday, & Company, N.Y. 1937.

1187. Martin, R.L., Cloninger, C.R., Guze, S.B. & Clayton, P.J. Mortality in a follow-up of 500 psychiatric outpatients. II. Cause-specific mortality. Arch Gen Psychiat. 1985, 42, 58-66.

1188. Martin, R.L., Cloninger, C.R. and Guze, S.B. Alcohol misuse and depression in women criminals. J Stud Alc. 1985, 46, 65-71.

1189. Martinius, J. Homicide of an aggressive adolescent boy with right temporal lesion: a case report. Neurosci Biobehav Rev. 1983, 7, 419-22.

1190. Massello, W., 3rd. The importance of clothing in death investigation--I. Med Leg Bull. 1983, 32, 1-6.

1191. Masumura, W.T. Law and violence: A cross-cultural study. J Anthropol Res. 1977, 33, 388-399.

1192. Masumura, W.T. Wife abuse and other forms of aggression. Victimology. 1979, 4, 46-59.

1193. Matheson, J.C.M. Infanticide. Med Leg Rev. 1941, 9, 135-152.

1194. Matheson, J.C. Alcohol and female homicides. Br J Inebr. 1939, 37, 87-90.

1195. Mathieson, D. & Passell, P. Homicide and robbery in New York City: an economic model. J Leg Stud. 1976, 5, 83-98.

1196. Matters, L. The Mystery of Jack the Ripper. Hutchinson Co., London, 1929.

1197. Matters, L. The Mystery of Jack the Ripper. W.H. Allen Co., London, 1948.

1198. Maughs, S.B. Criminal Psychopathology. In: Spiegel, E. (ed). Progress in Neurology and Psychiatry. Grune and Stratton, N.Y., 1970.

1199. Mawson, A.R. & Jacobs, K.W. Corn consumption, tryptophan, and cross-national homicide rates. J Orthomol Psychiat. 1978, 7, 227-230.

1200. May, A.E. An assessment of homicidal attitudes. Br J Psychiat. 1968, 114, 479-80.

1201. Mayfield, D. Alcoholism, alcohol, intoxication and assaultive behavior. Dis Nerv Sys. 1976, 37, 288-291.

1202. McCafferty, J. The value of firearms examination for the defense. Med Sci Law. 1981, 21, 170-4.

1203. McCarthy, J.B. Narcissism and the self in homicidal adolescents. Am J Psychoanal. 1978, 38, 19-29.

1204. McCarthy, J.D., Galle, O.R., Zimmern, W. Population density, social structure, and interpersonal violence: An intermetropolitan test of competing models. Am Behav Sci. 1975, 18, 771-791.

1205. McCarthy, V.O. Practical homicide investigation: tactics, procedures, and forensic technique. J Forens Sci. 1984, 1, 363-364.

1206. McClain, P.D. Black female homicide offenders and victims: Are they from the same population. Death Educat. 1982, 6, 265-78.

1207. McClain, P.D. Social and environmental characteristics of black female homicide offenders. West J Black Stud. 1981, 5, 224-30.

1208. McClain, P.D. Black females and lethal violence: Has time changed the circumstances under which they kill? Omega. 1982-83, 13, 13-25.

1209. McClain, P.D. Cause of death--homicide: A research note on black females as homicide victims. Victimology. 1982, 7, 204-212.

1210. McCormack, J. & McKinnery, W. Thallium poisoning in group assassination attempt. Postgrad Med. 1983, 74, 239-41, 244.

1211. McCormick, D. The Identity of Jack the Ripper. Pan Books Ltd., London, 1959.

1212. McCormick, D. The Identity of Jack the Ripper. John Long Co., London, 1970.

1213. McCully, R.S. Satan's eclipse: A familial murderer six years later. Br J Project Psychol Personal Stud. 1980, 25, 13-17.

1214. McCully, R.S. The laugh of Satan: a study of a familial murderer. J Person Assess. 1978, 42, 81-91.

1215. McDanal, C.E., Jr., & Siegel, B.L. An abused wife before and after filicide and suicide by her husband. Hawaii Med J. 1981, 40, 48.

1216. McDermaid, G. and Winkler, E.G. Psychiatric study of homicide cases. J Clin Psychopath. 1950, 11, 93-146.

1217. McDonald, A. & Patich, D. A study of homicide: the validity of predictive test factors. Can J Psychiat. 1981, 26, 549-54.

1218. McDonald, A. Homicide - constructive manslaughter. Crim Law Quart. 1982, 4, 402-412.

1219. McFarland, S.G. Is capital punishment a short-term deterrent to homicide? A study of the effects of four recent American executions. J Crim Law Criminol. 1983, 74, 1014-1032.

1220. McGovern, W.M., Jr. Homicide and succession to property. Mich Law Rev. 1969, 68, 65-110.

1221. McGurk, B.J. Personality types among "normal" homicides. Br J Criminol. 1978, 18, 146-161.

1222. McGurk, B.J. The validity and utility of a typology of homicides based on Megargee's theory of control. Personal Indiv Diff. 1981, 2, 129-136.

1223. McKee, C. Fantasies of mutiny and murder: A suggested psycho-history of the seaman in the United States Navy, 1798-1815. Armed Forces Soc. 1978, 4, 293-304.

1224. McKenna, J.J., Jablonski, N.G. & Fearnhead, R.W. A method of matching skulls with photographic portraits using landmarks and measurements of the dentition. J Forens Sci. 1984, 29, 787-97.

1225. McKnight, C.K., Mohr, J.W., Quinsey, R.E. and Erochko, J. Mental illness and homicide. Can Psychiat Assoc J. 1966, 11, 91-98.

1226. McKnight, C.K. Matricide and mental illness. Can Psychiat Assoc J. 1966, 11, 99-106.

1227. Mead, M. Cultural Factors in the Cause and Prevention of Pathological Homicide. In: MacDonald, J. (ed) Homicidal Threats. C.C. Thomas, Springfield, Ill, 1968.

1228. Medicott, R.W. Perverse tendencies and established victim-prone perversions. N.Z. Med J. 1985, 98, 147-50.

1229. Medicott, R.W. Psychiatric aspects of murder and attempted murder. N.Z. Med J. 1976, 83, 5-9.

1230. Medicott, R.W. The psychiatric aspects of violence. N.Z. Med J. 1980, 91, 181-4.

1231. Meerloo, J.A. The case of the murderous son. Am Practition. 1959, 10, 1109.

1232. Mehl, C.D. The mentally retarded in the criminal justice system: determining competency to stand trial. Diss Abs Intern. 1981, 42, 2069-B.

1233. Mehrotra, V.K. & Yadav, A.Y. Murder revealed by a broken piece of glass bangle: a case report. Med Sci Law. 1984, 24, 179-80.

1234. Meldman, J.A. Legal concepts of human life: The infanticide doctrines. Marquette Law Rev. 1968, 52, 105-115.

1235. Menninger, K. Murder. Bull Menninger Clin. 1973, 37, 305-20.

1236. Menninger, W.W. Threatening the President. Hosp Commun Psychiatr. 1982, 33, 436-7.

1237. Mercy, J.A. Homicide surveillance, 1970-1978. MMWR Surveill Summ. 1983, 32, 9SS-13SS.

1238. Merker, I. Dracon and early Athenian homicide law. Am J Legal Hist. 1984, 3, 288.

1239. Messner, S.F. Regional and racial effects on the urban homicide rate: The subculture of violence revisited. Am J Sociol. 1983, 88, 997-1007.

1240. Messner, S.F. Regional differences in the economic correlates of the urban homicide rate: Some evidence on the importance of cultural context. Criminology. 1983, 21, 477-488.

1241. Messner, S.F. Poverty, inequality, and the urban homicide rate. Criminology. 1982, 20, 103-114.

1242. Messner, S.F. Societal development, social equality, and homicide: A cross-national test of a Durkheimian model. Soc Forces. 1982, 61, 225-240.

1243. Mewett, A.W. First degree murder. Crim Law Quart. 1978, 21, 82-95.

1244. Mewett, A.W. Duress and mens rea. Crim Law Quart. 1975, 17, 352-354.

1245. Meyers, A.F., Sugar, C. and Apfelberg, B. Men who kill women. Part I., J Clin Psychopath Psychother. 1946, 7, 441-472.

1246. Meyers, H.P. An ecological study of southern homicide. Diss Abs Intern. 1980, 41, 1224.

1247. Meyers, Law Battered wives, dead husbands. Student Lawyer, 1978, 6, 46-51.

1248. Meyerson, A.T. Amnesia for homicide ("pedicide"). Its treatment with hypnosis. Arch Gen Psychiat. 1966, 14, 509-15.

1249. Michaels, J.J. Enuresis in murderous aggressive children and adolescents. Arch Gen Psychiat. 1961, 5, 490-3.

1250. Michalowski, R.J., Jr. Violence in the road: The crime of vehicular homicide. J Res Crim Delinq. 1975, 12, 30-43.

1251. Michaud, S.G. & Aunesworth, H. The Only Living Witness. Simon and Schuster, N.Y., 1983.

1252. Middleton, M. Tale told by a fly: entomologist solves murders. (Determination of species and stage of development of flies on dead bodies). Am Bar Assoc J. 1983, 571.

1253. Miethe, T.D. The impact of victim provocation on judgments of legal responsibility: An experimental assessment. J Crim Just. 1984, 12, 407-414.

1254. Miller, D. & Looney, J. The prediction of adolescent homicide: episodic dyscontrol and dehumanization. Am J Psychoanal. 1974, 34, 187-198.

1255. Miller, D. Psychodramatic ways of coping with potentially dangerous situations in psychotic and non-psychotic populations. Group Psychother Psychodrama. 1972, 25, 57-68.

1256. Miller, D. & Looney, J.G. Determinants of homicide in adolescents. Adolesc Psychiat. 1975, 4, 231-254.

1257. Miller, K., Moore, N. & Lexius, C. A group for families of homicide victims - an evaluation. J Contemp Soc Work. 1985, 66, 432-436.

1258. Miller, M.J., Miller, H.L., Davis, R.J. For whom does the bell toll? The true tragedy of the Atlanta youth murders. Am Psychol. 1983, 38, 229-230.

1259. Miller, R.D. The possible use of auto-hypnosis as a resistance during hyponotherapy. Int J Clin Exp Hypn. 1984, 32, 236-47.

1260. Milliken, A.D. Homicidal transsexuals: three cases. Can J Psychiat. 1982, 27, 43-6.

1261. Milne, H.B. Epileptic homicide: drug-induced. Br J Psychiat. 1979, 134, 547-8.

1262. Miloslavich, E.L. Forensic pathologic and criminalistic analysis of obscure murder cases. J Crim Law. 1952, 42, 689-93.

1263. Miloslavich, E.L. Uncommon criminal methods of infanticide. J Crim Law. 1951, 42, 414-16.

1264. Milstein, S. War is hell. It's also a good defense. Am Law. 1983, 9, 100-104.

1265. Miner, J.R. Nativity and parentage of the population of the United States and the homicide rate. Human Biol. 1929, 1, 274-278.

1266. Miner, J.R. Church membership and the homicide rate. Human Biol. 1929, 1, 562-564.

1267. Minty, L. Escape from the condemned cell on the eve of execution. Med Leg J. 1979, 47, 33-45.

1268. Minty, L.M. Murder as a fine art. Med Leg J. 1957, 25, 11-22.

1269. Mischke, P.E. Criminal law - homicide - self-defense - duty to retreat. Tenn Law Rev. 1982, 4, 1000-1023.

1270. Mitchell, E.J. & Holland, D. An usual case of identification of transferred fibers. J Forens Sci Soc. 1979, 19, 23-6.

1271. Mitchell, J. Race Riots in Black and White. Prentice-Hall, Englewood Cliffs, N J., 1970.

1272. Mitchell, M.H. Does wife abuse justify homicide? Wayne Law Rev. 1978, 24, 1705-1731.

1273. Moar, J.J. Homicide by dual modality. A case report. S Afr Med J. 1984, 65, 137-8.

1274. Moar, J.J. Determining the so-called moment of death in homicide victims. The significance of antemortem wounds and the postmortem interval. S Afr Med J. 1982, 62, 64-6.

1275. Modestin, J. & Boker, W. Homicide in a psychiatric institution. Br J Psychiat. 1985, 146, 321-4.

1276. Moffat, A.C. Forensic pharmacognosy-poisoning with plants. J Forens Sci Soc. 1980, 20, 103-9.

1277. Mohr, J.W. & McKnight, C.K. Violence as a function of age and relationship with special reference to matricide. Can Psychiat Assoc J. 1971, 16, 29-32.

1278. Monforte, J.R., Gault, R., Smialek, J. & Goodin, T. Toxicological and pathological findings in fatalities involving pentazocine and tripelennamine. J Forens Sci. 1983, 28, 90-101.

1279. Monforte, J.R. and Spitz, W.U. Narcotic abuse among homicide victims in Detroit. J Forens Sci. 1975, 20, 186-190.

1280. Moorman, C.B. Peace officers murdered in California 1973-1977. Awareness and learning points survey. J Calif Law Enforce. 1978, 13, 62-69.

1281. Moran, M.E. Physician-patient privilege prevents disclosure of patient's identity to grand jury homicide investigation. St John's Law Rev. 1984, 2.

1282. Moran, R. Criminal homicide: External restraint and subculture of violence. Criminology, 1971, 8, 357-374.

1283. Moreno, J.L. Note on indications and contra-indications for acting out in psychodrama. Group Psychother Psychodrama. 1973, 26, 23-24.

1284. Morris, N. & Hawkins, G. From Murder and from Violence, Good Lord, Deliver Us. In: Morris, N. (ed). The Honest Politician's Guide to Crime Control. Univ Chicago Press, Chicago, 1969.

1285. Morris, N. & Hawkins, G. From Murder and from Violence, Good Lord, Deliver Us. Midway, 1969, 10, 63-95.

1286. Morris, N. Corpus delicti and circumstantial evidence. Law Quart Rev. 1952, 68, 391-6.

1287. Morrison, G.C. Therapeutic intervention in a child psychiatry emergency service. J Am Acad Child Psychiat. 1969, 8, 542-558.

1288. Morrison, H.L. Psychiatric observations and interpretations of bite mark evidence in multiple murders. J Forens Sci. 1979, 24, 492-502.

1289. Morrison, W.A. Criminal homicide and the death penalty in Canada: Time for re-assessment and new directions: Toward a typology of homicide. Can J Criminol Correct. 1973, 15, 367-396.

1290. Morrison, H.L. Psychiatric observations and interpretations of bite mark evidence in multiple murders. J Forens Sci. 1979, 24, 492-502.

1291. Morrissy, E.P. A governmental face: formal and real mechanisms of conflict resolution in an antiviolent town. Aggress Behav. 1979, 5, 12-213.

1292. Morse, S.J. Diminished capacity: a moral and legal conundrum. Int J Law Psychiat. 1979, 2, 271-98.

1293. Morse, S.J. Undiminished confusion in diminished capacity. J Crim Law Criminol. 1984, 75, 1-55.

1294. Morton, J.H. Female homicides. J Ment Sci. 1934, 80, 64-74.

1295. Mulbar, Homicide Investigation; Practical Information for Coroners, Police Officers, and Other Investigators. C.C. Thomas, Springfield, Ill, 1956.

1296. Mullaly, P.R. Manslaughter by heat stroke. Med J Aust. 1976, 2, 926-7.

1297. Munford, R.S., Kazer, R.S., Feldman, R.A. & Stivers, R.R. Homicide trends in Atlanda. Criminology. 1976, 14, 2, 213-232.

1298. Murad, T.A. & Mertz, D. An analysis of a prehistoric homicide from northern California. J Forens Sci. 1985, 30, 948-52.

1299. Murdock, L.B. Malice aforethought. J Crim Law. 1934, 25, 454-7.

1300. Murphy, A.A. Suggested standard jury instructions on criminal homicide. Dick Law Rev. 1980, 1, 1-19.

1301. Murphy, G.K. The study of gunshot wounds in surgical pathology. Am J Forens Med Pathol. 1980, 1, 123-30.

1302. Murphy, G.K. The case of Stanley Setty. Am J Forens Med Pathol. 1980, 1, 245-7.

1303. Murphy, H.B.M. Current trends in transcultural psychiatry. Proc Roy Soc Med. 1973, 66, 711-716.

1304. Mushanga, T.M. Wife victimization in East and Central Africa. Victimology. 1978, 2, 479-485.

1305. Mutter, C.B. Regressive hypnosis and the polygraph: A case study. Am J Clin Hyp. 1979, 22, 47-50.

1306. Myers, S.A. Maternal filicide. Am J Dis Child. 1970, 534-6.

1307. Myers, S.A. The child slayer: A 25-year survey of homicides involving preadolescent victims. Arch Gen Psychiat. 1967, 17, 211-213.

N

1308 . Nagpaul, H. Patterns of homicide in north India -- Some sociological hypotheses. Int J Offend Ther Compar Criminol. 1985, 29, 147-158.

1309 . Namekata, T. "An epidemiologic study of homicides in Allegheny County, Pennsylvania". Am J Epidemiol. 1978, 108, 158-9.

1310 . Nash, J.R. Murder, America. Simon and Schuster, N.Y., 1980.

1311 . Nash, J. Death as a way of life: The increasing resort to homicide in a Mayan Indian community. Am Anthropol. 1967, 69, 455-470.

1312 . National Commission on the Cause and Prevention of Violence. Violent Crime: Homicide, Assault, Rape, Robbery. U.S. Government Printing Office, 1969.

1313 . National Commission on the Causes and Prevention of Violence. Violent Crime: Homicide, Assault, Rape, Robbery. George Braziller, N.Y., 1969.

1314 . Neithercutt, M.G. Parole violation patterns and commitment offense. J Res Crime Delinq. 1972, 9, 87-99.

1315 . Nelson, D.F. Petrol fires in closed rooms. J Forens Sci Soc. 1970, 10, 3-6.

1316 . Nemeth, C., Sosis, R.H. A simulated jury study: characteristics of the defendant the jurors. J Soc Psychol. 1973, 90, 221-229.

1317 . Nersesian. W.S., Petit, M.R., Shaper, R., Lemieux, D. & Naor, E. Childhood death and poverty: a study of all childhood deaths in Maine, 1976 to 1980. Pediatrics. 1983, 75, 41-50.

1318 . Neustatter, W.L. The Mind of the Murderer. Philosophical Library, N.Y., 1957.

1319 . Neustatter, W.L. The state of mind in murder. Lancet. 1965, 1, 861-3.

1320 . Newman, G.R. Acts, actors, and reactions to deviance. Sociol Soc Res. 1974, 58, 434-440.

1321 . Nichtern, S. The sociocultural and psychodynamic aspects of the acting-out and violent adolescent. Adolesc Psychiat. 1982, 10, 140-6.

1322 . Nissman, D.M., Barnes, B.R., Alpert, G.P., Beating the Insanity Defense: Denying the License to Kill. Lexington Books, Lexington, Mass. 1980.

1323 . Nixon, J., Pearn, J., Wilkey, I. & Petrie, G. Social class and violent child death: An analysis of fatal nonaccidental injury, murder, and fatal child neglect. J Child Abuse Negl. 1981, 5, 111-116.

1324 . Niyogi, S.K. Historic development of forensic toxicology in America up to 1978. Am J Forens Med Pathol. 1980, 1, 249-64.

1325 . Noguchi, T.T. & Nakamura, G.R. Phencyclidine-related deaths in Los Angeles County, 1976. J Forens Sci. 1978, 23, 503-7.

1326 . Norman, M.G. The postmortem examination on the abused child: Pathological, radiographic, and legal aspects. Perspect Pediat Pathol. 1984, 8, 313-343.

1327 . Norton, L.E., Garriott, J.C. & DiMaio, V.J. Drug detection at autopsy: a prospective study of 247 cases. J Forens Sci. 1982, 27, 66-71.

1328 . Novick, L.F. & Remminger, E. A study of 28 deaths in N.Y. City correctional facilities (1971-1976): implications for prisoner health care. Med Care. 1978, 16, 749-756.

1329. Nowak, M.K. Feticide in Illinois: legislative amelioration of a common law rule. North Ill Univ Law Rev. 1983, 1, 91-117.

1330. Nyman, T. Two aspects of new homicide law. Law Soc J. 1982, 6, 400.

O

1331 . Obeyesekere, G. Sorcery, premeditated murder, and the canalization of aggression in Sri Lanka. Ethnology. 1975, 14, 1, 1-23.

1332 . O'Connel, B. Amnesia and homicide. Br J Delinq. 1960, 10, 262-276.

1333 . O'Connor, J.F. & Lizotte, A. The "southern subculture of violence" thesis and patterns of gun ownership. Soc Probl. 1978, 25, 420-429.

1334 . Odesanmi, W.O. The fatal blood alcohol level in acute alcohol poisoning. Med Sci Law. 1983, 23, 25-30.

1335 . Offenkrantz, W., Tobin, A. & Freedman, R. An hypothesis about heroin addiction, murder, prostitution, and suicide: acting out parenting conflicts. Int J Psychoanal Psychother. 1978-79, 7, 602-8.

1336 . O'Hara, C.E. Fundamentals of Criminal Investigation, C.C. Thomas, Springfield, Ill, 1970, 853, 438-543.

1337 . Ojesjo, L. Alcohol, drugs, and forensic psychiatry. Psychiatr Clin North Am. 1983, 6, 733-49.

1338 . Oliver, J.S., Smith, H., & Watson, A.A. Poisoning by strychnine. Med Sci Law. 1979, 19, 134-7.

1339 . O'Malley, A. The Ethics of Medical Homicide and Mutilation. Devin-Adair Co., N.Y. 1919.

1340 . O'Neill, M.E. and Wilson, C.M. Homicide investigation kit. J Crim Law. 1940, 31, 357-63.

1341 . O'Neill, T.P. Murder least foul: A proposal to abolish voluntary manslaughter in Illinois. Ill Bar J. 1984, 6, 306-308.

1342 . O'Neill, T.P. "With malice toward none": a solution to an Illinois homicide quandary. De Paul Law Rev. 1982, 1, 107-126.

1343 . Orchard, G.F. Culpable homicide. N.Z. Law J. 1977, 411-15, 447-56.

1344 . O'Regan, R.S. Sorcery and homicide in Papau New Guinea. Aust Law J. 1974, 48, 76-82.

1345 . O'Regan, R.S. Indirect provocation and misdirected retaliation. Crim Law Rev. 1968, 319-324.

1346 . Osborne, H.W. Killing for profit -- the social-organization of felony homicide - Dietz ML. Soc Sci Quart. 1985, 66, 480-481.

1347 . Osborne, H.W. On crime, punishment, and deterrence. Soc Sci Quart. 1968, 49, 1, 157-160, 161-162.

1348 . Owens, C.E. Mental Health and Black Offenders. Lexington Books, Lexington, Massachusetts. 1980, 13-29.

1349 . Owsley, D.W., Mires, A.W. & Keith, M.S. Case involving differentiation of deer and human bone fragments. J Forens Sci. 1985, 30, 572-8.

P

1350. Pagan, D. & Smith, S.M. Homicide: a medico-legal study of thirty cases. Bull Am Acad Psychiat Law. 1979, 7, 275-85.

1351. Palframan, D.S. Two shootings. Can J Psychiat. 1979, 24, 61-4.

1352. Palinkas, L.A. Racial differences in accidental and violent deaths among U.S. Navy personnel. U.S. Naval Hlth Res Cent Rep. 1984, 84-45, 16.

1353. Palmer, C.H. and Weston, J.T. Several unusual cases of child abuse. J Forens Sci. 1976, 21, 851-855.

1354. Palmer, S. & Humphrey, J.A. Offender-victim relationships in criminal homicide followed by offender's suicide, North Carolina, 1972-1977. Suicide Life Threat Behav. 1980, 10, 106-18.

1355. Palmer, S. Sex differences in criminal homicide and suicide in England and Wales and the United States. Omega J Death Dying. 1980, 11, 3, 255-70.

1356. Palmer, S. The Violent Society. Yale University Press, New Haven, 1972.

1357. Palmer, S. Rebellion and Retreat. Charles E. Merrill, Columbus, Ohio, 1972, 109-126.

1358. Palmer, S. & Humphrey, J.A. Suicide and homicide: a test of a role theory of destructive behavior. Omega. 1977, 8, 45-58.

1359. Palmer, S. & Humphery, J.A. Familial and other relationships in criminal homicide in North Carolina. J Fam Iss. 1982, 3, 301-318.

1360. Palmer, S. Murder and suicide in 40 non-literate societies. J Crim Law Criminol Pol Sci. 1965, 56, 320-24.

1361. Palmer, S. The Psychology of Murder. Crowell, N.Y., 1962.

1362. Palmer, S. Frustration, aggression, and murder. J Abnorm Soc Psychol. 1960, 60, 430-2.

1363. Paluszny, M. & McNabb, M. Therapy of a 6-year-old who committed fratricide. J Am Acad Child Psychiat. 1975, 14, 319-336.

1364. Pancotti, J.J. Criminal law - confusion in the concept of criminal responsibility- the doctrine of diminished capacity and the use of mental impairment to reduce degree of conviction in Massachusetts. W New Eng Law Rev. 1981, 3, 583-603.

1365. Pankratz, L.D. Murder and insanity: 19th century perspectives from the "American Journal of Insanity." Int J Offend Ther Comp Criminol. 1984, 28, 37-43.

1366. Paris, J.J. & Reardon, F.E. Court responses to withholding or withdrawing artificial nutrition and fluids. JAMA. 1985, 253, 2243-5.

1367. Paris, R. Study of homicide. Can J Psychiat. 1982, 27, 258.

1368. Parker, E. The victims of mentally disordered female offenders. Br J Psychiat. 1974, 125, 51-59.

1369. Parker, N. Personality change following accidents. The report of a double murder. Br J Psychiat. 1980, 137, 401-9.

1370. Parker, N. Murderers: a personal series. Med J Aust. 1979, 1, 36-9.

1371. Parker, R.N. & Smith, M.D. Deterrence, poverty, and type of homicide. Am J Sociol. 1979, 85, 3, 614-624.

1372. Parker, N. Murderers: A personal series. Med J Aust. 1979, 1, 36-39.

1373. Parwatikar, S.D., Holcomb, W.R. & Menninger, K.A. The detection of malingered amnesia in accused murderers. Bull Am Acad Psychiat Law. 1985, 13, 97-103.

1374. Pasewark, R.A., Pantle, M.L. & Steadman, H.J. Characteristics and disposition of persons found not guilty by reason of insanity in N.Y. State, 1971-1976. Am J Psychiat. 1979, 136, 655-660.

1375. Pass, A.D. The MMPI personality profiles of murderers and other violent offenders. Diss Abs Intern. 1982, 43, 916.

1376. Pasternack, S.A. The American connection: Handguns and homicide. Med Ann Dist Col. 1973, 42, 369-373.

1377. Paternoster, R. Prosecutorial discretion in requesting the death penalty: A case of victim-based racial discrimination. Law Soc Rev. 1984, 18, 437-478.

1378. Paternoster, R. Race of victim and location of crime: The decision to seek the death penalty in South Carolina. J Crim Law Criminol. 1983, 74, 754-785.

1379. Patterson, R.M. Psychiatric study of juveniles involved in homicide. Am J Orthopsychiat. 1943, 13, 125-130.

1380. Perdue, W.C. & Lester, D. Racial differences in the personality of murderers. Percept Mot Skills. 1974, 38, 726.

1381. Perdue, W.C. & Lester, D. Those who murder kin: A Rorschach study. Percept Mot Skills. 1973, 36, 606.

1382. Perdue, W.C. Rorschach responses of 100 murderers. Correct Psychiat J Soc Ther. 1964, 10, 323-328.

1383. Perez, F.I. Behavioral analysis of clinical judgment. Percept Mot Skills. 1976, 43, 711-718.

1384. Perkins, R.M. Impelled perpetration restated. Hastings Law J. 1981, 2, 403-425.

1385. Perkins, R.M. The law of homicide. J Crim Law Criminol. 1946, 36, 391-454.

1386. Perloff, J.D., LeBailly, S.A., Kletke, P.R., Budetti, P.P., & Connelly, J.P. Premature death in the United States: years of life lost and health priorities. J Pub Hlth Policy. 1984, 5, 167-84.

1387. Pernanen, K. Alcohol and Crimes of Violence. In: Kissin, B. (ed). Social Aspects of Alcoholism. Plenum Press, N.Y., 1976.

1388. Perper, J.A. & Sobel, M.N. Identification of fingernail markings in manual strangulation. Am J Forens Med Pathol. 1981, 2, 45-8.

1389. Perr, I.N. The insanity defense: the case for abolition. Hosp Commun Psychiat. 1985, 36, 51-4.

1390. Pers, M.W. Infanticide: Past and present. W.W. Norton, N.Y., 1978.

1391. Petti, T.A. & Davidman, L. Homicidal school-age children: cognitive style and demograhic features. Child Psychiat Hum Dev. 1981, 12, 82-9.

1392. Pettigrew, T.F. & Spier, R.B. The Ecological Structure of Negro Homicide. In: Cohen, B. (ed). Crime in America. F.E. Peacock, Ithaca, Ill., 1970.

1393. Pettigrew, T.F. & Spier, R.B. Ecological pattern of negro homicide. Am J Sociol. 1962, 67, 621-629.

1394. Petursson, H. & Gudjonsson, G.H. Psychiatric aspects of homicide. Acta Psychiatr Scand. 1981, 64, 363-72.

1395. Pfeffer, C.R. Psychiatric hospital treatment of assaultive homicidal children. Am J Psychother. 1980, 34, 197-207.

1396. Phelps, H.A. Rhode Island's threat against murder. J Crim Law. 1928, 18, 552-67.

1397. Phillips, D.P. The impact of mass media violence in U.S. homicides. Am Sociol Rev. 1983, 48, 560-568.

1398. Phillips, D.P. Airplane accident fatalities increase just after newspaper stories about murder and suicide. Science. 1978, 201, 748-750.

1399. Phillips, D.P., Hensley, J.E. When violence is rewarded or punished: The impact of mass media stories on homicide. J Commun. 1984, 34, 101-116.

1400. Phillips, D.P. Strong and weak research designs for detecting the impact of capital punishment of homicide. Rutgers Law Rev. 1981, 3, 790-798.

1401. Phillips, D.P. The deterrent effect of capital punishment: New evidence on an old controversy. Am J Sociol. 1980, 86, 139-148.

1402. Phillips, L., Votey, H.L., Jr., and Howell, J. Handguns and homicide: minimizing losses and the costs of control. J Leg Stud. 1976, 5, 463-478.

1403. Picton, B. Murder, Suicide, or Accident; The Forensic Pathologist at Work. Hale, London, 1971.

1404. Piesiur, S.B., Strehlow, U. Poser, W. Increased mortality associated with dependence on legal drugs? Drug Alc Depend. 1984, 14, 97-99.

1405. Pirko, J.A. Defining the crime of excessive self-defense: voluntary manslaughter in Illinois. North Ill Univ Law Rev. 1982, 1, 217-234.

1406. Pitchandi, N. Forensic science in the homicide cases. Ind J Appl Psychol. 1969, 6, 100-102.

1407. Pittman, D.J. & Handy, W. Patterns in Criminal Aggravated Assault. In: Cohen, B. (ed). Crime in America. F.E. Peacock, Itasca, Illinois,, 1970.

1408. Pittman, D.J. & Handy, W. Patterns in criminal aggravated assault. J Crim Law Criminol. 1964, 55, 462-470.

1409. Planansky, K., Johnston, R. Homicidal aggression in schizophrenic men. Acta Psychiatr Scand. 1977, 55, 65-73.

1410. Pless, I.B. & Stulginskas, J. Accidents and violence as a cause of morbidity and mortality in childhood. Adv Pediatr. 1982, 29, 471-95.

1411. Podolsky, E. Jealous murderer. J Forens Med. 1965, 12, 35-40.

1412. Podolsky, E. Somnambulistic homicide. Am J Psychiat. 1964, 121, 191-2.

1413. Podolsky, E. Somnambulistic homicide. Med Sci Law. 1961, 1, 260.

1414. Podolsky, E. The lust murder. Ind Med J. 1961, 55, 81-3.

1415. Podolsky, E. Jealousy as a motive in homicide. Dis Nerv Syst. 1961, 22, 438-41.

1416. Podolsky, E. Somnambulistic homicide. Dis Nerv Syst. 1959, 20, 534-6.

1417. Podolsky, E. The manic murderer. Medicoleg J. 1959, 162-5.

1418. Podolsky, E. Notes on motiveless murder. Int J Soc Psychiat. 1956, 1, 42-45.

1419. Podolsky, E. Mind of the murderer. J Crim Law Criminol. 1954, 45, 58-50.

1420. Podolsky, E. The epileptic murderer. Medicoleg J. 1962, 30, 176-9.

1421. Podolsky, E. The electrophysiology of homicide. Dis Nerv Syst. 1962, 23, 146-8.

1422. Podolsky, E. The electrophysiology of homicide. J Forens Med. 1961, 8, 161-4.

1423. Podolsky, E. The psychodynamics of filicide and matricide. Dis Nerv Syst. 1958, 19, 475-7.

1424. Pokorny, A.D. Human Violence: A Comparison of Homicide, Aggravated Assault. In: Cohen, B. (ed). Crime in America, F.E. Peacock Publishers, Itasca, Ill., 1970.

1425. Pokorny, A.D. & Jachimczyk, J. The questionable relationship between homicides and the lunar cycle. Am J Psychiat. 1974, 131, 827-829.

1426. Pokorny, A.D. Human violence: A comparison of homicide, aggravated assault, suicide, and attempted suicide. J Crim Law Criminol. 1965, 56, 488-497.

1427. Pokorny, A.D. Homicide and weather. Am J Psychiat. 1963, 120, 806-8.

1428. Pokorny, A.D. Moon phases, suicide, and homicide. Am J Psychiat. 1964, 121, 66-7.

1429. Pokorny, A.D. A Comparison of Homicides in Two Cities. In: Cohen, B. (ed). Crime in America. F.E. Peacock, Ithaca, Illinois, 1970, 60-69.

1430. Pokorny, A.D. Sunspots, suicide, and homicide. Dis Nerv Syst. 1966, 27, 347-8.

1431. Pokorny, A.D. Geomagnetic fluctuations and disturbed behavior. J Nerv Ment Dis. 1966, 143, 140-51.

1432. Pokorny, A.D. A comparison of homicides in two cities. J Crim Law Criminol. 1965, 56, 479-487.

1433. Pollock, G.H. Manifestations of abnormal mourning: homicide and suicide following the death of another. Ann Psychoanal. 1976, 4, 225-249.

1434. Pontius, A.A. Specific stimulus-evoked violent action in psychotic trigger reactions: a seizure-like imbalance between frontal lob and limbic systems? Percept Mot Skills. 1984, 59, 299-333.

1435. Pontius, A.A. Stimuli triggering violence in psychoses. J Forens Sci. 1981, 26, 123-8.

1436. Porterfield, A.L. Indices of suicide and homicide by states and cities: some southern-non-southern contrasts with implications for research. Am Soc Rev. 1949, 14, 481-490.

1437. Post S. Adolescent parricide in abusive families. Child Welfare. 1982, 61, 445-55.

1438. Pound, R. Criminal Justice in America. Henry Holt and Co., N.Y.. 1930.

1439. Poussaint, A.F. Black-on-black homicide: A psychological-political perspective. Victimology. 1983, 8, 161-169.

1440. Powell, E. Society and homicide in the 13th century England. Mich Law Rev. 1981, 79, 967.

1441. Powell, E.H. Crime as a function of anomie. J Crim Law Criminol Pol Sci. 1966, 57, 161-171.

1442. Power, D.J. Paranoid psychosis and crime. Med Sci Law. 1968, 8, 105-108.

1443. Prathnadi, S. An successful murder. J Forens Sci. 1983, 28, 285-86.

1444. Precker, M.S. The treatment of juvenile offenders in murder cases. J Crim Law Criminol. 1950, 41, 49-54.

1445. Pride, D.E. Necrophilia complicating a case of homicide. Med Sci Law. 1963, 3, 121-31.

1446. Prins, H. Vampirism--a clinical condition. Br J Psychiat. 1985, 146, 666-8.

1447. Prins, H.A. Diminished responsibility and the Sutcliffe case: legal, psychiatric and social aspects (a 'layman's' view). Med Sci Law. 1983, 23, 17-24.

1448. Pritchard, D.H. Homicide and bargained justice: The agenda-setting effect of crime news on prosecutors. Diss Abs Intern. 1985, 45, 1904.

1449. Pruett, K.D. Home treatment for two infants who witnessed their mother's murder. J Am Acad Child Psychiat. 1979, 18, 647-57.

1450. Purver, J.M. Language of murder. UCLA Law Rev. 1967, 14, 1306.

1451. Pynoos, R.S., Eth, S. The child as witness to homicide. J Soc Iss. 1984, 40, 87-108.

Q

1452. Quinney, R. Suicide, homicide, and economic development. Soc Forces. 1965, 43, 401-406.

1453. Quinsey, V.L., Maguire, A. & Varney, G.W. Assertion and overcontrolled hostility among mentally disordered murderers. J Consult Clin Psychol. 1983, 51, 550-6.

R

1454. Radbill, S.X. A History of Child Abuse and Infanticide. In: R.E. Helfer and C.H. Kempe, (eds). The Battered Child. Univ Chicago Press, Chicago, 1974, 3-21.

1455. Radelet, M.L. Racial characteristics and the imposition of the death penalty. Am Sociol Rev. 1981, 46, 918-27.

1456. Raekallio, J. & Makinen, P.L. Biochemical reconstruction of three cases of death--results of international cooperation. J Forens Sci. 1978, 12, 25-32.

1457. Rao, V.J. & Hart, R. Tool mark determination in cartilage of stabbing victim. J Forens Sci. 1983, 28, 794-9.

1458. Rao, V.J., May, C.L., & DiMaio, V.J. The behavior of the expanding point .25 ACP ammunition in the human body. Am J Forens Med Pathol. 1984, 5, 37-9.

1459. Rappaport, E.A. Adolf Eichmann: The travelling salesman of genocide. Intern Rev Psychoanal. 1976, 3, 111-119.

1460. Rappaport, J. Implied malice must be proven to convict on a charge of assault with intent to commit murder. Pepperdine Law Rev. 1982, 4, 965-968.

1461. Rappeport, J.R. Gov. Wallace, Arthur Bremer and Dr. Rappeport, Part 1. Inside Arthur Bremer: Portrait of the Assailant. MD State Med J. 1978, 27, 35-8.

1462. Raschka, L.B. Lynching: a psychiatrist's view. Can Psychiatr Assoc J. 1976, 21, 577-80.

1463. Rascovsky, A. Filicide and the unconscious motivation for war. Adoles Psychiat. 1974, 3, 54-67.

1464. Rasko, G. The victim of the female killer. Victimology. 1976, 1, 396-402.

1465. Ratner, R.A. & Shapiro, D. The episodic dyscontrol syndrome and criminal responsibility. Bull Am Acad Psychiat Law. 1979, 7, 422-31.

1466. Raven, A. Theory of murder. Soc Rev. 1930, 22, 108-18.

1467. Raven. Murder and suicide as marks of an abnormal mind. Am Sociol Rev. 1929, 21, 315-333.

1468. Rawlins, G.C. An exploratory study of some psychological implications of the death penalty as measured on the MMPI of convicted murderers. Diss Abs Intern. 1976, 36, 5813-5814.

1469. Reay, D.T. & Eisele, J.W. Sexual abuse and death of an elderly lady by "fisting". Am J Forens Med Pathol. 1983, 4, 347-9.

1470. Reay, D.T. & Hazelwood, R.R. Death in military police custody and confinement. Milit Med. 1970, 135, 765-771.

1471. Reese, W.G. The major cause of death. J Arkansas Med Soc. 1970, 67, 155-159.

1472. Reik, T. The Unknown Murderer. Prentice-Hall, N.Y., 1945.

1473. Reinhardt, J.M. The Psychology of Strange Killers. C.C. Thomas, Springfield, Ill. 1962.

1474. Regan, S.G. Violent deaths among persons 15-24 years of age--United States, 1970-1978. Morbid Mortal Week Rep. 1983, 32, 453-457.

1475. Reich, P. & Hepps, R.B. Homicide during a psychosis induced by LSD. JAMA. 1972, 219, 869-871.

1476. Reid, J.D., Lee, E.S., Jedlicka, D. Shin, Y. Trends in black health. Phylon. 1977, 38, 105-116.

1477. Reinhardt, J.M. The dismal tunner: depression before murder. Intern J Offend Ther Comp Criminol. 1973, 17, 246-249.

1478. Reiser, M. Hypnosis as an aid in a homicide investigation. Am J Clin Hyp. 1974, 17, 84-87.

1479. Reppetto, T.A. The influence of police organizational style on crime control effectiveness. J Pol Sci Admin. 1975, 3, 274-279.

1480. Resnick, P.J. Child murder by parents: A psychiatric review of filicide. Am J Psychiat. 1969, 126, 73-82.

1481. Resnik, P.J. Murder of the newborn: a psychiatric review of neonaticide. Am J Psychiat. 1970, 126, 1414-20.

1482. Ressler, R.K., Burgess, A.W., & Douglas, J.E. Rape and rape-murder: one offender and twelve victims. Am J Psychiat. 1983, 140, 36-40.

1483. Restifo, N.P. & Lewis, D.O. Three case reports of a single homicidal adolescent. Am J Psychiat. 1985, 142, 388.

1484. Revitch, E. Patients who kill their physician. J Med Soc NJ. 1979, 76, 429-31.

1485. Revitch, E. & Schlesinger, L.B. Psychopathology of Homicide. C.C. Thomas, Springfield, Ill, 1981.

1486. Revitch, E. Sex murder and the potential sex murderer. Dis Nerv Syst. 1965, 26, 240-8.

1487. Reynolds, D.E. & Sanders, M.S. Effect of defendant attractiveness, age, and injury on severity of sentence given by simulated jurors. J Soc Psychol. 1975, 96, 149-150.

1488. Reynolds, M.M. Threats to confidentiality. Soc Work. 1976, 21, 108-113.

1489. Rhine, M.W. & Mayerson, P. A serious suicidal syndrome masked by homicidal threats. J Life Threat Behav. 1973, 3, 3-10.

1490. Rho, Y.M. Importance of examination of the clothed victim. Fingerprint identification of assailant from skin fragment on knifing victim's clothing. Am J Forens Med Pathol. 1985, 6, 19-20.

1491. Rice, D. Homicide from the perspective of NCHS statistics on blacks. Pub Hlth Rep. 1980, 95, 550-2.

1492. Richardson, O. Pattern criminal indictments, informations and jury instructions for Missouri -- some footnotes for a treatise. Missouri Bar J. 1979, 35, 18-37.

1493. Richman, J. Homicidal and Assaultive Behavior in the Elderly. In: B.L. Danto, J. Bruhan and G.H. Kutchen (eds). The Human Side of Homicide, Columbia Univ Press, N.Y. 1982.

1494. Richmond, F.C. Mental examination of fourteen-year-old boy parricide. Med Leg J. 1928-31, 47, 6-12.

1495. Riddick, L. & Luke, J.L. Alcohol-associated deaths in the District of Columbia--a postmortem study. J Forens Sci. 1978, 23, 493-502.

1496. Riedel, M. & Thornberry, T.P. Crime and Delinquency: Dimensions of Deviance. Praeger, N.Y., 1974.

1497. Riedel, M. & Brown, J. Perils and pitfalls of systems that collect data on homicide. Pub Hlth Rep. 1980, 95, 552.

1498. Rikard, M.G. Criminal law - the uncertain status of the felony-murder rule in Massachusetts. W New Eng Law Rev. 1984, 4, 1081-1101.

1499. Riley, D. & Cohen, H. Psychodynamics in a case of homicide. Intern J Offend Ther. 1977, 21, 26-30.

1500. Rinaldi, F. Negligent manslaughter. Crim Law J. 1984, 3, 190-192.

1501. Ritz, W. Felony murder transferred intent and the Palsgraf doctrine in the criminal law. Wash Lee Law Rev. 1959, 16, 169.

1502. Rivara, F.P. Traumatic deaths of children in the United States: Currently available prevention strategies. Pediatrics. 1985, 75, 456-462.

1503. Rizzo, N.D. Murder in Boston: Killers and their Victims. Intern J Offend Ther Compar Criminol. 1982, 26, 36-42.

1504. Roach, R.R. Medicine and killing: the Catholic view. J Med Philos. 1979, 4, 383-97.

1505. Roberson, C.E. Patterns of victim involvement in criminal homicide: a case study of San Francisco, California. Diss Abs Intern. 1976, 37, 1833.

1506. Roberts, G.B. Unlawful and dangerous act manslaughter. Monash Univ Law Rev. 1984, 228-231.

1507. Roberts, J.A. Criminal law - homicide - felony-murder - felon is culpable for murder in the first degree under Maryland's felony-murder statute when police officer kills kidnapped hostage used by felon as human shield. Univ Balt Law Rev. 1980, 3, 508-523.

1508. Robins, L.N. Negro homicide victims - who will they be. Trans Action. 1968, 5, 15-19.

1509. Rodenburg, M. Child murder by a depressed mother: a case report. Can Psychiatr Assoc J. 1971, 16, 49-53.

1510. Rodriguez, W.C., 3rd & Bass, W.M. Decomposition of buried bodies and methods that may aid in their location. J Forens Sci. 1985, 30, 836-52.

1511. Rogers, J.L., Sack, W.H., Bloom, J.D. & Manson, S.M. Women in Oregon's insanity defense system. J Psychiat Law. 1983, 11, 515-532.

1512. Rogers, R. & Seman, W. Murder and criminal responsibility: An examination of MMPI profiles. Behav Sci Law. 1983, 1, 89-95.

1513. Roizen, J. Alcohol and Criminal Behavior Among Blacks: The Case for Research on Special Populations. In: J.J. Collins, Jr. (ed). Drinking and Crime: Perspectives on the Relationships Between Alcohol Consumption and Criminal Behavior. Guilford Press, N.Y. 1981.

1514. Romero, L.M. Sufficiency of provocation for voluntary manslaughter in New Mexico: problems in theory and practice. New Mexico Law Rev. 1982, 2, 747-789.

1515. Roohanna, R.S. A survey of the psycho-social aspects of murderers in Iran. Forens Sci Int. 1982, 19, 51-66.

1516. Rosanoff, A.J. Thirty condemned men. Am J Psychiat. 1943, 99, 484-495.

1517. Rose, G.J. Screen memories in homicidal acting out. Psychoanal Quart. 1960, 29, 328-43.

1518. Rose, H.M. Lethal Aspects of Urban Violence: An overview. In: Rose, H.M. (ed). Lethal Aspects of Urban Violence. Lexington Books, Lexington, MA 1979, 1-16.

1519. Rose, H.M. The changing spatial dimension of black homicide in American cities. J Environ Sys. 1981, 11, 57-80.

1520. Rosenbaum, S.N. Israelite homicide law and the term "enmity" in Genesis 3:15. J Law Religion. 1984, 1, 145-151.

1521. Rosenblatt, E. and Greeland, C. Female crimes of violence. J Criminol Correct. 1974, 16, 173-180.

1522. Rosenblatt, P.C. Grief and involvement in wrongful death litigation. Law Hum Behav. 1983, 7, 351-359.

1523. Rosenfeld, L. Alfred Swaine Taylor (1806-1880), pioneer toxicologist--and a slight case of murder. Clin Chem. 1985, 31, 1235-6.

1524. Rosenzweig, S., Simon, B. and Ballou, M. The psychodynamics of an uxoricide. Am J Orthopsychiat. 1942, 12, 283-294.

1525. Roslund, B. & Larson, C.A. Crimes of violence and alcohol abuse in Sweden. Int J Addict. 1979, 14, 1103-15.

1526. Rosner, R., Wiederlight, M., Rosner, M.B. & Wieczorek, R.R. Adolescents accused of murder and manslaughter: a five-year descriptive study. Bull Am Acad Psychiat Law. 1979, 7, 342-51.

1527. Roth, N.E., Sundby, S.E. The felony-murder rule: a doctrine at constitutional crossroads. Cornell Law Rev. 1985, 3, 446-492.

1528. Rotton, J., Kelly, I.W. & Frey, J. Geophysical variables and behavior: X detecting lunar periodicities: something old, new, borrowed, and true. Psychol Rep. 1983, 52, 111-6.

1529. Roughead, W. Murderer's Companion. Norton, N.Y., 1968.

1530. Roulston, R.P. Sentencing a juvenile for manslaughter. Aust N Z J Criminol. 1968, 1, 174-156.

1531. Rowe, W.F. Discussion of "George Armstrong Custer and the Battle of the Little Bighorn: homicide or mass suicide". J Forens Sci. 1984, 29, 696-9.

1532. Ruben, E.R. & Leeper, J.D. Homicide in five southern states: a firearms phenomenon. South Med J. 1981, 74, 272-7.

1533. Rubin, P.J. Homicide. Main Law Rev. 1976, 28, 57-63.

1534. Rudnick, S.A. The identification of a murder victim using a comparison of the postmortem and antemortem records. J Forens Sci. 1984, 29, 349-54.

1535. Rumbelow, D. The Complete Jack the Ripper. N.Y. Graphic Society, Boston, 1975.

1536. Rummel, B. The right of law enforcement officers to use deadly force to effect an arrest. N.Y. Law Forum. 1968, 14, 749-762.

1537. Ruotolo, A.K. Neurotic pride and homicide. Am J Psychoanal. 1975, 35, 1-16.

1538. Ruotolo, A.K. Dynamics of sudden murder. Am J Psychoanal. 1968, 28, 162-76.

1539. Rushforth, N.B., Ford, A.B., Hirsch, C.S., Rushforth, N.M., Adelson, L. Violent death in a metropolitan county: Changing patterns in homicide (1958-74). New Engl J Med. 1977, 297, 531-538.

1540. Russell, D.H. Juvenile murderers. Intern J Offend Ther Comp Criminol. 1973, 17, 235-239.

1541. Russell, L.G. Psycho-social characteristics of homicide victims and suicide victims. Diss Abs Intern. 1981, 42, 1237-B.

1542. Rynearson, E.K. Bereavement after homicide: a descriptive study. Am J Psychiat. 1984, 141, 1452-4.

S

1543. Sadoff, R.L. LSD, alcohol, and homicide. JAMA. 1973, 225, 1123.

1544. Sadoff, R.L. Clinical observations on parricide. Psychiat Quart. 1971, 45, 65-9.

1545. Sagarin, E. & Macnamara, D.E.J. The homosexual as a crime victim. Intern J Criminol Penol. 1975, 3, 13-25.

1546. Sagarin, E. Corrections: Problems of and Rehabilitation. Praeger, N.Y.,. 1973, 154, 106-114.

1547. Sal, F.T. Regional viewpoints on population growth: perspectives of the genocide issue. Int J Hlth Serv. 1973, 3, 753-8.

1548. Salzman, L. Psychodynamics of a case of murder. Comprehens Psychiat. 1962, 3, 152-169.

1549. Sampson, R.J. Race & criminal violence: A demographically disaggregated analysis of urban homicide. J Crime Delinq. 1985, 31, 47-82.

1550. Samuels, A. Mental illness and criminal liability. Med Sci Law. 1975, 15, 198-204.

1551. Sander, R., Ryser, M.A., Lamoreaux, T.C. & Raleigh, K. An epidemic of cocaine associated deaths in Utah. J Forens Sci. 1985, 30, 478-84.

1552. San Marco, L.R. Differential sentencing patterns among criminal homicide offenders in Harris County, Texas. Diss Abs Intern. 1979, 40, 3550-A.

1553. Saravanapavananthan, N. Homicide by burning. Ceylon Med J. 1981, 26, 84-5.

1554. Sargent, D. Children Who Kill -- A Family Conspiracy. In: Howells, J. (ed). Theory and Practice of Family Psychiatry. Brunner/Mazel, N.Y., 1971, 734-744.

1555. Satten, J., Menninger, K., Rosen, I. and Mayman, M. Murder without apparent motive: a study in personality disorganization. Am J Psychiat. 1960, 117, 48-53.

1556. Sauer, N.J. & Simson, L.R. Clarifying the role of forensic anthropologists in death investigations. J Forens Sci. 1984, 29, 1081-6.

1557. Saunders, J.M. A clinical study of widow bereavement involving various modes of death. Diss Abs Intern. 1980, 40, 5606-B.

1558. Sayed, Z.A., et al. An electroencephalographic and psychiatric study of thirty-two insane murderers. Br J Psychiat. 1969, 115, 1115-24.

1559. Schachter, M. Attempts to homicide and homicides committed by subjects under 20 years: Clinical and psychodiagnostic investigations. Acta Paedopsychiat. 1975, 41, 174-187.

1560. Schapera, I. Some anthropological concepts of crime. Br J Sociol. 1972, 23, 381-394.

1561. Schetky, D.H. Children and handguns. A public health concern. Am J Dis Child. 1985, 139, 229-31.

1562. Schetky, D.H. Preschoolers' responses to murder of their mothers by their fathers: a study of four cases. Bull Am Acad Psychiat Law. 1978, 6, 45-47.

1563. Schilder, P. Attitude of murderers toward death. J Abnorm Psychol. 1936, 31, 348-63.

1564. Schipkowensky, N. Adolescent murderers through love. Acta Paedopsychiat. 1975, 41, 187-202.

1565. Schipkowensky, N. Affective disorders: cyclophrenia and murder. Int Psychiat Clin. 1968, 5, 59-75.

1566. Schmalzbach, O.R. Attempted homicide under drug influence: superman of the supermarket. Aust J Forens Sci. 1981, 1, 2-8.

1567. Schmid, D.F. Study of homicides in Seattle, 1914 to 1924. Soc Forces. 1926, 4, 745-56.

1568. Schmidt, K., Hill, L. & Guthrie, G. Running amok. Intern J Soc Psychiat. 1977, 23, 264-274.

1569. Schmidt, O.H., Reitz, J.A. and Spitz, W.U. Peculiarities of certain .22 caliber revolvers (Saturday night specials). J Forens Sci. 1974, 19, 48-53.

1570. Schneck, J.M. Hypnotic relief of guilt associated with murder of a parent. Intern J Eclectic Psychother. 1983, 2, 10-17.

1571. Schuh, C. Justice on the northern frontier: early murder trials of native accused. Crim Law Quart. 1979, 22, 74-111.

1572. Schur, E.M. Poverty, Violence, and Crime in America. In: Schur, E. (ed). Our Criminal Society. Prentice Hall, Englewood Cliffs, N.J. 1969, 121-157.

1573. Schwade, E.D. and Otto, O. Infanticide as manifestation of thalamic or hypothalamic disorder with abnormal electroencephalographic findings. Wisc Med J. 1953, 52, 171-174.

1574. Schwartz, D.W. Some problems in predicting dangerousness. Psychiat Quart. 1980, 52, 79-83.

1575. Schwendinger, H. & Schwendinger, J.R. The continuing debate on the legalistic approach to the definition of crime. Iss Criminol. 1972, 7, 71-81.

1576. Scobie, A. Murder for Magic; Witchcraft in Africa. Cassell, London, 1965.

1577. Scott, E.M. Violence in America: violent people and violent offenders. Intern J Offend Ther Compar Ther. 1979, 23, 197-209.

1578. Scott, E.M. The act of murder. Intern J Offend Ther Comp Criminol. 1975, 19, 154-163.

1579. Scott, P.D. Offenders, drunkenness and murder. Br J Addict. 1968, 63, 221-226.

1580. Scott, P.D. Parents who kill their children. Med Sci Law. 1973, 13, 120-6.

1581. Seiden, R.H. & Freitas, R.P. Shifting patterns of deadly violence. J Suicide Life Threat Behav. 1980, 10, 195-209.

1582. Seitz, S.T. Firearms homicides and gun control effectiveness. Law Soc Rev. 1972, 6, 595-613.

1583. Selke, W.L. & Pepinsky, H.E. The politics of police reporting in Indianapolis, 1948-1978. Law Hum Behav. 1982, 6, 327-342.

1584. Selkin, J. Rescue fantasies in homicide-suicide. J Suicide Life Threat Behav. 6, 79-85, 1977.

1585. Sellin, T. Is murder increasing in Europe? Ann Am Acad Pol Soc Sci. 1926, 125, 29-34.

1586. Sellin, T. The basis of a crime index. J Crim Law Criminol. 1931, 22, 335-336.

1587. Sellin, T. The measurement of criminality in geographic areas. Proceed Am Philosoph Soc. 1953, 97, 163-167.

1588. Senay, E.C. & Wettstein, R. Drugs and homicide: a theory. Drug Alc Depend. 1983, 12, 157-66.

1589. Sendi, I.B. & Blomgren, P.G. A comparative study of predictive criteria in the predisposition of homicidal adolescents. Am J Psychiat. 1975, 132, 423-427.

1590. Sethi, B.B. Rorschach as a measure of psychopathology in murder. Ind J Psychiat. 1971, 13, 243-247.

1591. Shaffer, D.R. & Case, T. On the decision to testify in one's own behalf: Effects of withheld evidence, defendant's sexual preferences, and juror dogmatism on juridic decisions. J Personal Soc Psychol. 1982, 42, 335-346.

1592. Shagoury, P.B. An exploratory investigation of homicidal behavior. Diss Abs Intern.

1593. Shaler, R.C. Interpretation of Gm testing results: two case histories. J Forens Sci. 1982, 27, 231-5.

1594. Shaler, R.C. A multi-enzyme electrophoretic system for the identification of seminal fluid from postmortem specimens. Am J Forens Med Pathol. 1981, 2, 315-21.

1595. Shapiro, H.A. Arsenic content of human hair and nails: its interpretation. J Forens Med. 1967, 14, 65-71.

1596. Sharman, R.L. Child death resulting from non-accidental injury: implications for health visitors. Nurs Times. 1982, 78, 242-5.

1597. Sharman, R.L. Homicide among black males. Pub Hlth Rep. 1980, 95, 549.

1598. Shaw, R.S. Murderers who repeat. N Engl J Med. 1970, 282, 1435.

1599. Sheehan-Dare, H. Homicide during a schizophrenic episode. Int J Psychoanal. 1955, 36, 43-52.

1600. Sheehy, E.A. Criminal law: homicide, working paper no. 33. Can Bar Rev. 1985, 2, 435-442.

1601. Sheley, J.F. & Ashkins, C.D. Crime, crime news, and crime views. Pub Opin Quart. 1981, 45, 492-506.

1602. Shelley, L.I. Crime and modernization: The impact of industrialization and urbanization on crime. Southern Illinois Univ, Carbondale, Ill, 1981.

1603. Shelton, J.L., Sanders, R.S. Mental health intervention in a campus homicide. J Am College Hlth Assoc. 1973, 21, 346-50.

1604. Shenken, L.I. The implications of ego psychology of a motiveless murder. J Am Acad Child Psychiat. 1964, 3, 741-41.

1605. Sheppard, C. Towards a better understanding of the violent offender. Can J Criminol Correct. 1971, 13, 60-67.

1606. Sheridan, E.P. & Teplin, L.A. Recidivism in difficult patients: Differences between community mental health center and state hospital admissions. Am J Psychiat. 1981, 138, 688-690.

1607. Sherman, L.W. Execution without trial: police homicide and the constitution. Vand Law Rev. 1980, 1, 71-100.

1608. Sherman, L.W. and Langworthy, R.H. Measuring homicide by police officers. J Crim Law Criminol. 1979, 70, 546-560.

1609. Shew, E.S. Companion to Murder. A. Knopf, N.Y., 1961.

1610. Shew, E.S. A Second Companion to Murder; A Dictionary... 1900-1950. Cassell, London, 1960, 286.

1611. Shin, Y., Jedlicka, D. & Lee, E.S. Homicide among blacks. Phylon. 1977, 38, 398-407.

1612. Shoham, S. Points of no return: Some situational aspects of violence. Prison J. 1968, 48, 29-33.

1613. Sholder, J.M. Murder scene warrantless searches: a proposal. Arizona Law Rev. 1979, 21, 777-793.

1614. Shore, J.H. Psychiatric epidemiology among American Indians. Psychiatr Ann. 1974, 4, 56-66.

1615. Showalter, C.R. & Bonnie, R.J. Psychiatrists and capital sentencing: risks and responsibilities in a unique legal setting. Bull Am Acad Psychiat Law. 1984. 12, 159-67.

1616. Showalter, C.R., Bonnie, R.J. & Roddy, V. The spousal-homicide syndrome. Intern J Law Psychiat. 1980, 3, 117-41.

1617. Shupe, L.M. Alcohol and crime. A study of the urine alcohol concentration found in 882 persons arrested during or immediately after the commission of a felony. J Crim Law Criminol Pol Sci. 1954, 44, 661-664.

1618. Shupe, L.M. Ethyl alcohol in blood and urine. Am J Clin Pathol. 1952, 22, 901-910.

1619. Shuster, S. Jack the Ripper and doctor-identification. Intern J Psychiat Med. 1975, 6, 385-402.

1620. Siegler, R. Medical complicity in the Guyana tragedy. N Engl J Med. 1979, 301, 559.

1621. Sikes, R.K. Alcohol and fatal injuries--Fulton County, Georgia, 1982. Morbid Mortal Week Rep. 1983, 32, 573-576.

1622. Silver, B.J., Goldston, S.E., & Silver, L.B. The 1990 objectives for the nation for control of stress and violent behavior: progress report. Pub Hlth Rep. 1984, 99, 374-84.

1623. Silverman, R.A. & Teevan, J.J. Crime in Canadian Society. Butterworth, Toronto, 1975, 455.

1624. Simon, R.H. & Desilva, M. Intracranial tuberculoma coexistent with uncinate seizures and violent behavior. JAMA. 1981, 245, 1247-8.

1625. Simon, R.I. Type A, AB, B murderers: their relationship to the victims and to the criminal justice system. Bull Am Acad Psychiat Law. 1977, 5, 344-62.

1626. Sims, B.G. Homicide and the dentist. Med Leg J. 1980, 48, 25-43.

1627. Singh, A. A study of the personality and adjustment of murderers. Ind J Clin Psychol. 1979, 6, 201-204.

1628. Skinner, R.E. Narcotics, barred windows, and murder: the medical practitioner in the writings of Raymond Chandler. Perspect Biol Med. 1983, 27, 127-34.

1629. Skolnick, J.H. A study of the relation of ethnic background to arrests for inebriety. Quart J Stud Alc. 1954, 622-630.

1630. Slater, H.W. On the etiology of criminal homicides - the alcohol factor. J Pol Sci Adm. 1974, 2, 50-53.

1631. Smale, D. Heavy mineral studies as evidence in a murder case in outback Australia. J Forens Sci Soc. 1969, 9, 123-8.

1632. Smart, R.G. & Bateman, K. Unfavorable reactions to LSD: A review and analysis of the available case reports. Can Med Assoc J. 1967, 97, 1214-1221.

1633. Smialek, J.E., Spitz, W.U., & Wolfe, J.A. Ethanol in intracerebral clot. Report of two homicidal cases with prolonged survival after injury. Am J Forens Med Pathol. 1980, 1, 149-50.

1634. Smialek, J.E. Accidental death with tear as pen gun: a case report. J Forens Sci. 1975, 20, 708-13.

1635. Smith, A.T.H. The provoked drunk. Mod Law Rev. 1981, 9, 567-571.

1636. Smith, C.G. Ward meetings in a security hospital. Bull Am Acad Psychiat Law. 1978, 6, 458-67.

1637. Smith, J.L. Police inspection and complaint reception procedures. F.B.I. Law Enforce Bull. 1974, 43, 12-15.

1638. Smith, M.D., Parker, R.N. Type of homicide and variation in regional rates. Soc Forces. 1980, 59, 1, 136-147.

1639. Smith, R. The state of the prisons. Deaths in prison. Br Med J [Clin Res]. 1984, 288, 208-12.

1640. Smith, R. Scientific thought and the boundary of insanity and criminal responsibility. Psychol Med. 1980, 10, 15-23.

1641. Smith, S.M. Competency. Psychiatr Clin North Am. 1983, 6, 635-50.

1642. Smith, S.M., & Braun, C. Necrophilia and lust murder: report of a rare occurrence. Bull Am Acad Psychiat Law. 1978, 6, 259-68.

1643. Smith, S. The adolescent murderer. A psychodynamic interpretation. Arch Gen Psychiat. 1965, 13, 310-9.

1644. Smykal, A. and Thorne, F.C. Etiological studies of psychopathic personality. II. Asocial type. J Clin Psychol. 1951, 7, 299-316.

1645. Smythe, J.G., Jr. Mississippi's parricide statute. Miss Law J. 1931, 4, 132-4.

1646. Snow, C.C., Levine, L., Lukash, L, Tedeschi, L.G., Orrego, C. & Stover, E. The investigation of the human remains of the "disappeared" in Argentina. Am J Forens Med Pathol. 1984, 5, 297-9.

1647. Snyder, L. Homicide investigation; practical information for coroners, police officers, and other investigators. C.C. Thomas, Springfield, Ill., 1944.

1648. Sobell, L.C. & Sobell, M.B. Alcohol and drug use by alcohol and drug abusers when incarcerated: Clinical and research implications. Addict Behav. 1983, 8, 89-92.

1649. Sobell, L.C. Drunkenness, A "special circumstance" in crimes of violence: Sometimes. Intern J Addict. 1975, 10, 869-882.

1650. Solheim, T. Unusual dental forensic cases in Norway. Am J Forens Med Pathol. 1980, 1, 197-203.

1651. Solomon, A.E. Evidence - minors have no privilege to refuse to testify against their parents. Suffolk Univ Law Rev. 1984, 4, 835-843.

1652. Solomon, G.F. Capital punishment as suicide and as murder. Am J Orthopsychiat. 1975, 45, 701-711.

1653. Solomon, K. The masculine gender role and its implications for the life expectancy of older men. J Am Geriat Soc. 1981, 29, 297-301.

1654. Solomon, P. The burden of responsibility in suicide and homicide. JAMA. 1967, 199, 99-102.

1655. Solursh, L.P. Psychoactive drugs, crime and violence. Psychol Rep. 1975, 37, 1177-1178.

1656. Somasundaram, O. Depressive illness and crime. Ind J Criminol. 1979, 7, 153-156.

1657. Somers, A.R. Violence, television and the health of American youth. N Engl J Med. 1976, 294, 811-6.

1658. Somogyi, E. The history of forensic medicine in Hungary. Am J Forens Med Pathol. 1985, 6, 145-7.

1659. Sorrels, J., Jr. What can be done about juvenile homicide? J Crime Delinq. 1980, 26, 152-61.

1660. Sorrells, J.M. Kids who kill. J Crime Delinq. 1977, 23, 312-20,

1661. Spain, D.M., Bradess, V.A. and Eggston, A.A. Alcohol and violent death. A one-year study of consecutive cases in a representative community. JAMA. 1951, 146, 334-335.

1662. Sparrow, G. The Great Assassins. Longmans, London, 1968.

1663. Sparrow, G. Women who Murder. Barker, London, 1970.

1664. Spencer, J.D. George Armstrong Custer and the Battle of the Little Bighorn: homicide or mass suicide? J Forens Sci. 1983, 28, 756-61.

1665. Spencer, J.D. Medical examiner/coroner jurisdiction in cases involving federal interests. J Forens Sci. 1982, 27, 408-11.

1666. Sperber, N.D. Chewing gum-an unusual clue in a recent homicide investigation. Int J Orthod. 1981, 19, 7-8.

1667. Sperber, N.D. Chewing gum: An unusual clue in a recent homicide investigation. J Forens Sci. 1978, 23, 792-796.

1668. Spitz, W.U. & Fisher, R.S. Medicolegal Investigation of Death. C.C. Thomas. Springfield, Ill., 1973.

1669. Sprague, H.B. The murder of the penultimate Puritan. p. 50-71. Trans Assoc Am Physic. 1958, 71.

1670. Stack, S. Homicide and property crime: The relationships to anomie. Aggress Behav. 1983, 9, 339-344.

1671. Stack, S. Comment on Krohn's "Inequality, unemployment and crime: A cross-national analysis". Soc Quart. 1978, 19, 340-342.

1672. Stanton, J.M. Murderers on parole. J Crime Delinq. 1969, 15, 149.

1673. Staples, R. To be young, black and oppressed. Black Scholar. 1975, 7, 2-9.

1674. Starrs, J.E. Procedure in identifying fingernail imprint in human skin survives appellate review. Am J Forens Med Pathol. 1985, 6, 171-3.

1675. Steadman, H.J., Pasewark, R.A., Hawkins, M., Kiser, M. & Bieber, S. Hospitilization length of insanity acquittees. J Clin Psychol. 1983, 39, 611-14.

1676. Stearns, A.W. Homicide in Massachusetts. Amer J Psychiat. 1925, 4, 725-749.

1677. Steele, W.W., Jr. & Hill, B. A legislative proposal for a legal right to die. Crim Law Bull. 1976, 12, 140-164.

1678. Stein, K.B. Correlates of the ideational preference dimension among prison inmates. Psychol Rep. 1967, 21, 553-562.

1679. Steinmetz, S.K. & Straus, M.A. The family as cradle of violence. Trans Action. 1973, 10, 50-56.

1680. Stern, M. Study of unsolved murders in Wisconsin from 1924-1928. J Crim Law. 1931, 21, 513-36.

1681. Stevens, R.L. A president's assassination. JAMA. 1981, 246, 1673-4.

1682. Stewart, G.W. Felony murder in Texas: the merger problem. Baylor Law Rev. 1981, 4, 1035-1043.

1683. Stewart, W. Jack the Ripper: A New Theory. Quality Press, London, 1939.

1684. Stowell, T.E.A. Jack the Ripper--A solution? Criminologist. 1970, 5, 4.

1685. Stratton, R. Relationship between prevalence of alcohol problems and socioeconomic conditions among Oklahoma Native Americans. Curr Alc. 1981, 8, 315-25.

1686. Strohm, R.B. & Wolfgang, M.E. Relationship between alcohol and criminal homicide. Quart J Stud Alc. 1956, 17, 411-425.45

1687. Stroud, D.A. Constructive murder and drunkenness. Law Quart Rev. 1920, 268.

1688. Stumberg, G.W. Criminal homicide in Texas. Texas Law Rev. 1938, 16, 305-34.

1689. Sturner, W.Q. and Garriot, J.C. Comparative toxicology in vitreous humor and blood. Can Soc Forens Sci. 1975, 8, 126-131.

1690. Sturup, G.K. The psychology of murderers. J Irish Med Ass. 1964, 54, 27-32.

1691. Sutker, P.B., Allain, A.N. & Geyer, S. Female criminal violence and differential MMPI characteristics. J Consult Clin Psychol. 1978, 46, 1141-3.

1692. Sutker, P.B. & Moan, C.E. A psychosocial description of penitentiary inmates. Arch Gen Psychiat. 1973, 29, 663-667.

1693. Suval, E.M. & Brisson, R.C. Neither beauty or beast: female criminal homicide offenders. Intern J Criminol Penol. 1974, 2, 23-34.

1694. Svalastoga, K. Homicide and social contact in Denmark. Am J Social 1956, 62, 37-41.

1695. Swartz, C.M. Managing desperate emotional behaviour with hypnosis. Can J Psychiat. 1981, 26, 555-557.

1696. Swezey, R.W. Estimating drug-crime relationships. Intern J Addict. 1973, 8, 701-721.

1697. Swigert, V.L. & Farrell, R.A. Normal homicides and the law. Am Sociol Rev. 1977, 42, 16-32.

1698. Swigert, V.L., Farrell, R.A. & Yoels, W.C. Sexual homicide: social, psychological, and legal aspects. Arch Sex Behav. 1976, 5, 391-401.

1699. Swigert, V.L. & Farrell, R.A. Speedy trial and the legal process. Law Hum Behav. 1980, 4,135-145.

1700. Swigert, V.L. & Farrell, R.A. Corporate homicide: Definitional processes in the creation of deviance. Law Soc Rev. 1980-81, 15, 161-182.

1701. Sylvester, S.F., Reed, J.H. & Nelson, D.O. Prison Homicide. Spectrum Publications, N.Y.,1977, 149.

1702. Symonds, M. Neurotic pride and homicide. Am J Psychoanal. 1975, 35, 17-18.

1703. Szasz, T.S. Psychosis, psychiatry and homicide. JAMA. 1972, 220, 864-865.

T

1704. Tabakman, M. Forensic medical service in the U.S.S.R. Am J Forens Med Pathol. 1980, 1, 271-6.

1705. Tahourdin, B. Life sentence prisoners: Deterioration and coping. Intern J Offend Ther Comp Criminol. 1980, 24, 241-243.

1706. Tamura, M. Characteristics and typology of recent criminal homicide. Rep Nat Res Inst Pol Sci. 1983, 24, 78-90.

1707. Tamura, M. Changes in the patterns of criminal homicide for recent three decades. Rep Nat Res Inst Pol Sci. 1983, 24, 149-161.

1708. Tan, E.K. & Carr, J.E. Psychiatric sequelae of Amok. Cult Med Psychiat. 1977, 1, 59-67.

1709. Tanay, E. The Murderers. Bobbs-Merrill, N.Y.1976, 169.

1710. Tanay, E. Adolescents who kill parents: Reactive parricide. Aust N.Z. J Psychiat. 1973, 7, 263-277.

1711. Tanay, E. Psychiatric aspects of homicide prevention. Am J Psychiat. 1972, 128, 815-818.

1712. Tanay, E. Psychiatric study of homicide. Am J Psychiat. 1969, 125, 1252-1257.

1713. Taney, E. Family violence. J Forens Sci. 1984, 29, 820-4.

1714. Taney, E. Psychodynamic differentiations of homicide. Bull Am Acad Psychiat Law. 1978, 6, 364-73.

1715. Taney, E. Reactive parricide. J Forens Sci. 1976, 21, 76-82.

1716. Tardiff, K. Patterns and major determinants of homicide in the United States. Hosp Commun Psychiat. 1985, 36, 632-639.

1717. Tasso, J. & Miller, E. The effects of the full moon on human behavior. J Psychol. 1976, 93, 81-83.

1718. Taylor, P.J. & Gunn, J. Violence and psychosis. I. Risk of violence among psychotic men. Br Med J [Clin Res]. 1984, 288, 1945-9.

1719. Taylor, P.J., & Kopelman, M.D. Amnesia for criminal offenses. Psychol Med. 1984, 14, 581-8.

1720. Taylor, R.M. Cranial evidence of attack with intent to kill. N.Z. Dent J. 11978, 74, 215-7.

1721. Taylor, R.L. & Weisz, A.E. American Presidential Assassination. In: Daniels, D. (ed). Violence and the Struggle for Existence. Little, Brown, Boston, 1970, 451, 291-307.

1722. Tennessee Department of Mental Health and Mental Retardation. Homicide and suicide as leading causes of decreasing life expectancy of young Black males. J Tenn Med Assoc. 1978, 71, 117-118.

1723. Tentori, T. & Chiauzzi, G. On sororicide/filiacide for family honour. Curr Anthropol. 1981, 22, 300-301.

1724. Teuteur, W. Murder and attempted murder--practical hints for psychiatric testimony. J Forens Sci. 1964, 9, 492-500.

1725. Theis, W.H. Preliminary hearings in homicide cases: A hearing delayed is a hearing denied. J Crim Law Criminol Pol Sci. 1971, 62, 17-28.

1726. Thom, D.A. Juvenile delinquency and criminal homicide. J Maine Med Assoc. 1949, 40,176-180.

1727. Thomas, C.W. Homicide among black males. Final observations and summary. Pub Hlth Rep. 1980, 95, 560-1.

1728. Thomas, G.E. Fatal .45-70 rifle wounding of a policeman wearing a bulletproof vest. J Forens Sci. 1982, 27, 445-9.

1729. Thomson, I.G. Homicide and suicide in Africa and England. Med Sci Law. 1980, 20, 99-103.

1730. Thomson, W.A.R. Urban violence in the USA. Med Sci Law. 1984, 1, 68-69.

1731. Thornton, W.E. & Pray, B.J. The portrait of a murderer. Dis Nerv Sys. 1975, 36, 176-178.

1732. Ting, S.K. Post-mortem survey of homicides in Singapore (1955-1964). Singapore Med J. 1969, 10, 243-7.

1733. Ting, T.Y. Planning for the prevention of juvenile delinquency in the Philippines. Law Critique. 1970, 36, 13-16.

1734. Tinklenberg, J.R. Alcoholism and Violence. In: Bourne, P.G. (ed). Alcohol Prog Res Treat. Academic Press, N.Y., 1973, 195-210.

1735. Tinklenberg, J.R. and Stillman, R.C. Drug Use and Violence. In: D.N. Daniels, (ed). Violence and the Struggle for Existence. Little, Brown & Co., Boston, 1974, 327-365.

1736. Tittle, C.R. Crime rates and legal sanctions. Soc Prob. 1969, 16, 409-413.

1737. Toch, H. Violent men: An Inquiry into the Psychology of Violence. Aldine, Chicago, 1969, 26.

1738. Tooley, K. The small assassins: Clinical notes on a subgroup of murderous children. J Am Acad Child Psychiat. 1975, 14, 306-318.

1739. Tosayanond, S. Homicide: a study at Siriraj Hospital, Bangkok. Med Sci Law. 1984, 24, 222-6.

1740. Tosto, D.D. The battered spouse syndrome as a defense to a homicide charge under the Pennsylvania Crimes Code. Vill Law Rev. 1980, 1, 105-134.

1741. Totman, J., The murderess: A psychosocial study of the process of criminal homicide. Diss Abs Intern. 1971, 31, 6726.

1742. Totman, J.M. The Murderess: A Psychosocial study of the Process of Criminal Homicide. Univ California Press, Berkeley, Cal. 1970.

1743. Totty, R.N. A case of handwriting on an unusual surface. J Forens Sci Soc. 1981, 21, 349-50.

1744. Towers, B. Irreversible coma and withdrawal of life support: is it murder if the IV line is disconnected? J Med Ethics. 1982, 8, 203-5.

1745. Trafford, P.A. Homicide in acute porphyria. J Forens Sci. 1976, 7, 113-20.

1746. Treitel, G.H. Nervous shock and homicide. Law Quart Rev. 1954, 70, 168-9.

1747. Tresher, R.L. and O'Neill, T.N. Medical care for dependent children: Manslaughter liability of the Christian Scientist. Univ Pa Law Rev. 1960, 109, 203.

1748. Trexler, R.C. Infanticide in Florence: New sources and first results. Hist Childhood Quart. 1973, 1, 98-116.

1749. Trott, L., Barnes, G. & Dumoff, R. Ethnicity and other demographic characteristics as predictors of sudden drug-related deaths. J Stud Alc. 1981, 42, 564-78.

1750. Trunkey, D.D. Trauma care systems. Emerg Med Clin North Am. 1984, 2, 913-22.

1751. Trunkey, D.D. Shock trauma. Can J Surg. 1984, 27, 479-86.

1752. Tucker, L.S., Cornwall, T.P. Mother-son folie a deaux: A case of attempted patricide. Am J Psychiat. 1977, 134, 1146-1147.

1753. Tulchin. Intelligence and Crime. Univ Chicago Press, Chicago. 1939, 39-41.

1754. Turk, A.T. The mythology of crime in America. Criminology. 1971, 8, 397-411.

1755. Turns, D.M. & Gruenberg, E.M. An attendant is murdered: The state hospital responds. Psychiat Quart. 1973, 47, 487-494.

1756. Turner, C.W., Fenn, M.R. & Cole, A.M. A Social Psychological Analysis of Violent Behavior. In: Stuart, R. (ed). Violent Behavior. Brunner/Mazel, N.Y., 1981, 303, 31-67.

1757. Turner, C. Fears of genocide among black Americans as related to age, sex, and region. J Pub Hlth. 1973, 63, 1029-34.

1758. Tushnet, L. The weight of evidence. JAMA 1970, 212, 137-8.

1759. Tuter, W. and Glotzer, J. Murdering mothers. Am J Psychiat. 1959, 116, 447-52.

1760. Tuteur, W. Further observations on murdering mothers. J Forens Sci. 1966, 11, 373-83.

U

1761. Ueshima, H., Cooper, R., Stamler, J., Yu, C., Tatara, K. & Asakura, S. Age specific mortality trends in the U.S.A. from 1960 to 1980: divergent age-sex-color patterns. J Chron Dis. 1984, 37, 425-39.

1762. Uglow, S. Implied malice and the Homicide Act of 1957. Mod Law Rev. 1983, 2, 164-177.

1763. Uhlin, D.M. The use of drawings for psychiatric evaluation of a defendant in a case of homicide. Ment Hlth Soc. 1977, 4, 61-73.

1764. Unnithan, N.P. Homicide and the social structure: A cross-national analysis of lethal violence rates, 1950-1970. Diss Abs Intern. 1984, 44, 2591.

1765. Usher, A. The contribution of the defense pathologist. Med Sci Law. 1980, 20, 246-9.

1766. U.S. Justice Department Criminal Division. Firearms Facts. U.S. Department of Justice, Washington, D.C. 1968.

V

1767. Vale, G.L. & Noguchi, T.T. Anatomical distribution of human bite marks in a series of 67 cases. J Forens Sci. 1983, 28, 61-9.8

1768. Valente, C.M. Patterns of suicide and homicide in Prince George's county, Maryland: 1971-1980. Diss Abs Intern. 1983, 44, 1794-1795.

1769. Van Hecke, W. A case of murder by parathion (E 605) which nearly escaped detection. Med Sci Law. 1964, 4, 197-9.

1770. Van-Manen, G.C. Macrostructural Sources of Variation in Homicide Victim Rates in the Capital City. In: Viano, E.C. (ed). Victims and Society. Visage, Washington, DC, 1976, 255-267.

1771. Vargas, L.A. Early bereavement in the four modes of death in whites, blacks, and hispanics. Diss Abs Intern. 1983, 43, 3746.

1772. Varma, L.P. Characteristics of murder in mental disorder. Am J Psychiat. 1966, 122, 1296-8.

1773. Venker, P.N. Missouri homicides: lesser included offenses and instructing down. Missouri Law Rev. 1983, 4, 935-981.

1774. Verberne, T.J.P. Blackburn's typology of abnormal homicides: Additional data and a critique. Br J Criminol. 1972, 12, 88-89.

1775. Verbrugge, L.M. Recent trends in sex mortality differentials in the United States. Women Hlth. 1980, 5, 17-37.

1776. Vigderhous, G. Suicide and homicide as causes of death and their relationship to life expectancy: A cross-cultural comparison. Soc Biol. 1975, 22, 338-343.

1777. Vigderhous, G. Sociodemographic determinants of suicide and homicide--A multivariate cross-cultural investigation. Diss Abs Intern. 1975, 36, 3154-3155.

1778. Vigderhous, G. Methodological problems confronting cross-cultural criminological research using official data. Hum Relat. 1978, 31, 229-247.

1779. Vinson, T. Homicides and serious assaults in New South Wales. Anglo-Amer Law Rev. 1974, 3, 29-36.

1780. Vinson, T. & Marshall, C. Crime in our cities: A comparative study. Aust J Soc Iss. 1973, 8, 201-208.

1781. Virkkunen, M. Serum cholesterol levels in homicidal offenders. A low cholesterol level is connected with a habitually violent tendency under the influence of alcohol. Neuropsychobiol. 1983, 10, 65-9.

1782. Virkkunen, M. Suicide linked to homicide. Psychiat Quart. 1974, 48, 276-282.

1783. Virkkunen, M. Alcohol as a factor precipitating aggression and conflict behaviour leading to homicide. Br J Addict. 1974, 69, 149-154.

1784. Von Hentig, H. Pre-murderous kindness and post-murder grief. J Crim L. 1957, 48, 368.

1785. Voss, H.L. & Hepburn, J.R. Patterns in criminal homicide in Chicago. J Crim Law Criminol Pol Sci. 1968, 59, 499-508.

W

1786. Wade, J.W. Acquisition of property by willfully killing another: a statutory solution. Harv Law Rev. 1936, 49, 715-55.

1787. Waegel, W.B. Patterns of police investigation of urban crimes. J Pol Sci Admin. 1982, 10, 452-465.

1788. Wagih, I.M. A biometrical and medico-legal assessment of homicide in Alexandria (1965-1968). J Egypt Med Assoc. 1970. 53, 722-9.

1789. Wagner, E.E. & Klein, I. WAIS differences between murderers and attackers referred for evaluation. Percept Mot Skills. 1977, 44, 125-126.

1790. Wagner, S. Woman's right, physician's judgment: Commonwealth v. Edelin and a physician's criminal liability for fetal manslaughter. Women's Rights Law Report. 1978, 4, 97-114.

1791. Waldron, I. & Eyer, J. Socioeconomic causes of the recent rise in death rates for 15-24 yr-olds. Soc Sci Med. 1975, 9, 383-396.

1792. Walker, A.E. Murder or epilepsy? J Nerv Ment Dis. 1961, 133, 430-7.

1793. Wallace, E.R, 4th. The primal parricide. Bull Hist Med. 1980, 54, 153-65.

1794. Wallace, S.E. Patterns of Violence in San Juan. In: Dinitz, S. (ed). Deviance. Oxford Univ Press, N.Y., 1969, 62-67.

1795. Walsh, B.K.S. Children who have murdered. Med Leg J. 1975, 43, 20-24.

1796. Walsh, B.K.S. Psychopathology of homicidal children. Roy Soc Hlth J. 1974, 274-277.

1797. Walsh, M.N. A contribution to the problem of recurrent mass homicide. J Hillside Hosp. 1966, 15, 84-93.

1798. Walsh-Brennan, K.S. An analysis of homicide by young persons in England and Wales. Acta Psychiatr Scand. 1976, 54, 92-8.

1799. Walsh-Brennan, K.S. Children who have murdered. Med Leg J. 1975, 43, 20-4.

1800. Walsh-Brennan, K.S. Child murderers: an analysis. Criminologist. 1974, 9, 3-12.

1801. Walshe, B.K.S. A socio-psychological investigation of young murderers. Br J Criminol. 1977, 17, 58-63.

1802. Walter, R. Homosexual panic and murder. Am J Forens Med Pathol. 1985, 6, 49-51.

1803. Walter, R.A. An examination of the psychological aspects of bite marks. Am J Forens Med Pathol. 1984, 5, 25-9.

1804. Ward, D.A., Jackson, M. & Ward, R.E. Crimes of Violence by Women. In: Mulvihill, D. (ed). Crimes of Violence. Government Printing Office, Washington, 1969, 843-909.

1805. Warren, C.W., Smith, J.C. & Tyler, C.W. Seasonal variation in suicide and homicide: a question of consistency. J Biosoc Sci. 1983, 15, 349-56.

1806. Wasserman, I.M. The linkage of United States presidential elections, unemployment changes, and reductions in suicide, accident, and homicide rates. J Soc Psychol. 1984, 124, 115-7.

1807. Wasserman, I.M. Non-deterrent effect of executions of homicide rates. Psychol Rep. 1981, 48, 137-8.

1808. Wasserman, I.M. Religious affiliations and homicide: Historical results from the rural south. J Scient Stud Relig. 1978, 17, 415-418.

1809. Wasserman, K.T. Case study of an intriguing "primitive" murder trial: financial settlement between the murderer and the victim's family. Bull Am Acad Psychiat Law. 1981, 9, 275-84.

1810. Weiss, J.M. Lamberti, J.W. and Blackman, N., The sudden murderer. A comparative analysis. Arch Gen Psychiat. 1960, 2, 669-78.

1811. Weissman, J.C. Imposing homicide liability for death-producing drug law violations. West Law Rev. 1975, 12, 102-121.

1812. Weisz, A.E. & Taylor, R.L. American presidential assassinations. Dis Nerv Sys. 1969, 30, 659-668.

1813. Weller, M. Violence and mental illness. Br Med J [Clin Res]. 1984, 289, 2-3.

1814. Wellman, M.W. Dead and Gone. Univ North Carolina Press, Chapel Hill, 1955.

1815. Wells, C. Look hard and see more. Mod Law Rev. 1984, 1, 98-103.

1816. Wells, C. Criminal law revision committee, 14th report: offenses against the person: homicide. Mod Law Rev. 1980, 6, 681-691.

1817. Wertham, F. The Show of Violence. Doubleday, Garden City, NY. 1949.

1818. Wertham, F. The matricidal impulse: critique of Freud's interpretation of Hamlet. J Crim Psychopath. 1941, 2, 455-464.

1819. West, D.J. A note on murders in Manhattan. Med Sci Law. 1968, 8, 249-55.

1820. Westermeyer, J. Mortality and psychosis in a peasant society. J Nerv Ment Dis. 1978, 166, 769-74.

1821. Westermeyer, J., Neider, J., Stone, B., & Bearman, J. Alcoholism indicators: nonreliability of events partially related to alcohol abuse. Am J Drug Alc Abuse. 1982-83, 9, 333-44.

1822. Westermeyer, J. On the epidemicity of Amok violence. Arch Gen Psychiat. 1973, 28, 873-6.

1823. Westermeyer, J. A comparison of Amok and other homicide in Laos. Am J Psychiat. 1972, 129, 703-709.

1824. Westermeyer, J. & Brantner, J. Violent death and alcohol use among the Chippewa in Minnesota. Minn Med. 1972, 55, 749-752.

1825. Westermeyer, J. & Peake, E. A ten-year follow-up of alcoholic native Americans in Minnesota. Am J Psychiat. 1983, 140, 189-194.

1826. Westermeyer, J. Grenade-amok in Laos: A psychosocial perspective. Intern J Soc Psychiat. 1973, 19, 251-260.

1827. Westermeyer, J. Assassination and conflict resolution in Laos. Am Anthropol. 1973, 75, 123-131.

1828. Wetli, C.V. Investigation of drug-related deaths: An overview. Am J Forens Med Pathol. 1984, 5, 111-120.

1829. Wetli, C.V. Changing patterns of methaqualone abuse. A survey of 246 fatalities. JAMA. 1983, 249, 621-6.

1830. Wexler, D.B. An offense-victim approach to insanity defense reform. Ment Physic Disabil Law Rep. 1984, 8, 146-149.

1831. Whitt, H.P., Gordon, C.C. & Hofley, J.R. Religion, economic development and lethal aggression. Am Sociol Rev. 1972, 37, 193-201.

1832. Whitt, H.P. The lethal aggression rate and the suicide-murder ratio: A synthetic theory of suicide and homicide. Diss Abs. 1969, 29, 2624-2625.

1833. Whittington, R.M. Alcohol-related deaths: Birmingham Coroner's records 1980. Br Med J [Clin Res]. 1982, 284, 1162.

1834. Widom, C.S. An empirical classification of female offenders. Crim Just Behav. 1978, 5, 35-52.

1835. Wiecking, D.K. Cases from the morgue. Va Med. 1985, 112, 306-9.

1836. Wigmore, J.H. Identification of bullet and firearm. Ill Law Rev. 1931, 25, 692-3.

1837. Wilbanks, W. Trends in violent death among the elderly. Int J Aging Hum Dev. 1981-82, 14, 167-75.

1838. Wilbanks, W. A test of Verkko's static and dynamic "Laws" of sex and homicide. Intern J Women's Stud. 1981, 4, 173-180.

1839. Wilbanks, W. Female homicide offenders in the U.S. Intern J Women's Stud. 1983, 6, 302-310.

1840. Wilbanks, W. Fatal accidents, suicide and homicide: Are they related? Victimology. 1982, 7, 213-217.

1841. Wilbanks, W. Is violent crime intraracial? J Crime Delinq. 1985, 31, 117-128.

1842. Wilbanks, W. Does alcohol cause homicide? J Crime Just. 1981, 15, 149-170.

1843. Wilbanks, W. Homicide victimization rates in Dade County, Florida. Victimology. 1979, 4, 305-307.

1844. Wilber, C.G. Medicolegal investigation of the President John F. Kennedy murder. C.C. Thomas, Springfield, Ill., 1978.

1845. Wilbur, M.P. Vietnam: Completing the emotional sequence. Person Guid J. 1984, 62, 280-284.

1846. Wilcox, D.E. The relationship of mental illness to homicide. Am J Forens Psychiat. 1985, 6, 3-15.

1847. Wilentz, W.C. and Brady, J.P. The alcohol factor in violent deaths. Am Practit 1961, 12, 829-35.

1848. Wilkey, I., Pearn, J. Petrie, G. & Nixon, J. Neonaticide, infanticide and child homicide. Med Sci Law. 1982, 22, 31-4.

1849. Wilkinson, K.P. A research note on homicide and rurality. Soc Forces. 1984, 63, 445-452.

1850. Wilkinson, D.Y. Social Structure and Assassination Behavior: The Sociology of Political Murder. Schenkman, Cambridge, MA, 1976.

1851. Wille, W.S. Citizens who Commit Murder: A Psychiatric Study. Warren H. Green, St. Louis, 1975.

1852. William, J.E.H. Psychopath and the defense of diminished responsibility. Mod Law Rev. 1958, 31, 544.

1853. Williams, A.H. A psychoanalytic approach to the treatment of the murderer. Int J Psychoanal. 1960, 41, 532-539.

1854. Williams, G. Constructive malice revived. Mod Law Rev. 1960, 23, 605.

1855. Williams, G. Causation in homicide. Crim Law Rev. 1957, 429, 510.

1856. Williams, G. Provocation and the reasonable man. Crim Law Rev. 1954, 740-54.

1857. Williams, K.R. Economic sources of homicide: reestimating the effects of poverty and inequality. Am Sociol Rev. 1984, 49, 283-9.

1858. Williams, L.N. Causation - death caused either by push or by stabbing supposed corpse - whether conviction for manslaughter possible. Crim Law Rev. 1981, 493-494.

1859. Williams, L.N. Causation - doctors switching off life-support machine - injury still an operating cause - withdrawal of question from jury. Crim Law Rev. 1981, 401-403.

1860. Williams, L.N. Intention to cause serious bodily harm - whether sufficient mens rea. Crim Law Rev. 1981, 180-181.

1861. Williams, L.N. LSD and manslaughter. Lancet 1969, 2, 332.

1862. Williams, M. Blacks and alcoholism: Issues in the 1980's. Alc Hlth Res W. 1982, 6, 31-40.

1863. Willis, J. Manslaughter by the intentional infliction of some harm: a category that should be closed. Crim Law J. 1985, 2, 109-124.

1864. Wilmer, H.A. "Murder, you know". Psychiat Quart. 1969, 43, 414-47.

1865. Wilson, C.L. Examination of Ripper handwriting. Criminologist. 1974-1975, 9, 48.

1866. Wilson, R.A., Ratledge, E.C., Malin, H.J. General indicators of alcohol-related mortality for United States counties. Adv Alc Subst Abuse. 1982, 2, 41-52.

1867. Wilt, G.M. Domestic violence and the police: studies in Detroit and Kansas City. Police Foundation, Washington, DC, 1977.

1868. Wingersky, M.F. Death by definition. De Paul Law Rev. 1958, 7, 172.

1869. Winkler, E.G. and Train, G.J. Acts of violence with electroencephalographic changes. J Clin Exp Psychopath. 1959, 20, 223-30.

1870. Winkler, G.E., Kove, S.S. The implications of electroencephalographic abnormalities in homicide cases. J Neuropsychiat. 1962, 3, 322-30.

1871. Wise, P.H., Kotelchuck, M., Wilson, M.L. & Mills, M. Racial and socioeconomic disparities in childhood mortality in Boston. New Engl J Med. 1985, 313, 360-6.

1872. Wolf, A.S. Homicide and blackout in Alaskan natives: a report and reproduction of five cases. J Stud Alc. 1980, 41, 456-62.

1873. Wolf, A.S. Alcohol and violence in the Alaskan native: A follow-up and theoretical considerations. Alc Treat Quart. 1984, 1, 133-138.

1874. Wolfgang, M.E. Victim Precipitated Criminal Homicide. In: Patterson, D. (ed). Crime and Criminal Justice, MSS Information Corp. N.Y., 1974, 149, 80-90.

1875. Wolfgang, M.E. Victim Precipitated Criminal Homicide. In: Drapkin, I. (ed). Victimology. Lexington Books, Lexington Mass. 1974, 79-92.

1876. Wolfgang, M.E. Sociological Factors in Homicide. In: Palmer, S. (ed). Rebellion and Retreat. Charles E. Merrill, Columbus, Ohio, 1972, 95-108.

1877. Wolfgang, M.E. Victim Precipitated Criminal Homicide. In: Wolfgang, M. (ed). The Sociology of Crime and Delinquency, John Wiley and Sons, N.Y., 1970, 569-578.

1878. Wolfgang, M.E. A Sociological Analysis of Criminal Homicide. In: Cohen, B. (ed). Crime in America. F.E. Peacock. Itasca, Illinois, 1970, 52-60.

1879. Wolfgang, M.E. Victim Precipitated Criminal Homicide. In: Cohen, B. (ed). Crime in America. F.E. Peacock, Itasca, Illinois, 1970, 456-464.

1880. Wolfgang, M.E. & Cohen, B. The Victims of Crime. In: Wolfgang, M. (ed). Crime and Race: Conceptions and Misconceptions. Institute of Human Relations Press, N.Y., 1970, 40-56.

1881. Wolfgang, M.E. & Ferracuti, F. The Subculture of Violence. In: Wolfgang, M. (ed). The Sociology of Crime and Delinquency, John Wiley and Sons, N.Y., 1970, 676, 380-391.

1882. Wolfgang, M.E. & Ferracuti, F. Subculture of Violence: An Integrated Conceptualization. In: Arnold, D. (ed). The Sociology of Subcultures. The Glendessary Press, Berkeley, 1970, 171, 135-149.

1883. Wolfgang, M.E. & Ferracuti, F. The Subculture of Violence. Tavistock, London. 1967

1884. Wolfgang, M.E. Victim precipitated criminal homicide. J Crim Law Criminol Pol Sci. 1957, 48, 1-11.

1885. Wolfgang, M.E. The relationship between alcohol and criminal homicide. Quart J Stud Alc. 1956, 17, 411-425.

1886. Wolfgang, M.E. Patterns of Criminal Homicide. W. Saunders, Phil. 1958.

1887. Wolfgang, M.E. Husband-wife homicides. J Soc Ther. 1956, 2, 263-271.

1888. Wolfgang, M.E. Subculture of Violence: Towards an Integrated Theory in Criminology. Barnes & Noble, N.Y., 1967.

1889. Wolfgang, M.E. Studies in Homicide. Harper & Row, N.Y. 1967.

1890. Wolin, S.S. Violence and the western political tradition. Am J Orthopsychiat. 1963, 33, 15-28.

1891. Wong, M. & Singer, K. Abnormal homicide in Hong Kong. Br J Psychiat. 1973, 123, 295-298.

1892. Wood, A.L. A socio-structural analysis of murder, suicide and economic crime in Ceylon. Am Sociol Rev. 1961, 26, 744-753.

1893. Wright, J.A. & Kelly, D.H. Race, socioeconomic status, the dangerous person, and the disposition severity of juvenile homicide cases. Calif Sociologist. 1984, 7, 129-158.

1894. Wright, R.K. and Davis, J. Homicidal hanging masquerading as sexual asphyxia. J Forens Sci. 1976, 21, 387-389.

1895. Wright, R.K. and Davis, J.H. Studies in the epidemiology of murder: a proposed classification system. J Forens Sci., 1977, 22, 464-470.

Y

1896. Yadav, R.A. Women who kill -- an exploratory study of the institutionalized homicide female offenders. Ind J Clin Psychol. 1976, 3, 121-123.

1897. Yager, J. Personal violence in infantry combat. Arch Gen Psychiat. 1975, 32, 257-261.

1898. Yates, A., Beutler, L.E. & Crago, M. Characteristics of young, violent offenders. J Psychiat Law. 1983, 11, 137-149.

1899. Yearwood, J.H. Firearms and Interpersonal Relationships in Homicide: Some Cross-National Comparisons. In: M. Riedel & T.P. Thornberry (ed). Crime and Delinquency: Dimensions of Deviance. Praeger, N.Y., 1974.

1900. Young, V.D. Victims of Female Offenders. In: W.H. Parsonage (ed). Perspectives on Victimology. Sage Publications, Beverly Hills, 1975, 73-87.

1901. Yunker, J.A. Testing the deterrent effect of capital punishment: A reduced form approach. Criminology. 1982, 19, 626-649.

Z

1902. Zahn, M.A. The female homicide victim. Criminology. 1975, 13, 400-415.

1903. Zahn, M.A. & Bencivengo, M. Violent death: A comparison between drug users and nondrug users. Addict Dis. 1974, 1, 283-295.

1904. Zeanah, C.H. & Burk, G.S. A young child who witnessed her mother's murder: therapeutic and legal considerations. Am J Psychother. 1984, 38, 132-45.

1905. Zeegers, M. Violence between intimate partners: case-histories and commentary. Int J Law Psychiat. 1982, 5, 431-8.

1906. Zeidenrust, J. Fatal phosphorous poisoning elucidated by exhumation three and a half years after burial. Med Sci Law. 1964, 4, 120-1.

1907. Zeisel, H. A comment on "the deterrent effect of capital punishment" by Phillips. Am J Sociol. 1982, 88, 167-169.

1908. Zeiss, C.A. Hypothesis on sexual violence "not convincing". Am J Psychiat. 1984, 141, 1133.

1909. Zenoff, E.H. & Zients, A.B. Juvenile murderers: should the punishment fit the crime? Int J Law Psychiat. 1979, 2, 533-53.

1910. Zimring, F.E., Mukherjee, S.K. & Van-Winkle, B. Intimate violence: a study of intersexual homicide in Chicago. Univ Chi Law Rev. 1983, 2, 910-930.

1911. Zimring, F. Is gun control likely to reduce violent killings. Univ Chi Law Rev. 1968, 35, 721-737.

1912. Zimring, F.E. Determinants of the death rate form robbery: A Detroit time study. J Leg Stud. 1977, 6, 317-332.

1913. Zimring, F.E. Games with guns and statistics. Wisc Law Rev. 1968, 1113-1126.

1914. Zimring, F.E., Eigen, J. & O'Malley S. Punishing homicide in Philadelphia: perspectives on the death penalty. Univ Chi Law Rev. 1976, 43, 227-252.

1915. Zimring, F.E. Youth homicide in New York: A preliminary analysis. J Leg Stud. 1984, 13, 1, 81-99.

1916. Zonana, H.V. Hypnosis, sodium amytal, and confessions. Bull Am Acad Psychiat Law. 1979, 7, 18-28.

1917. Zugibe, F.T. & Costello, J.T. Identification of a murder weapon by a peculiar blunt force injury pattern and histochemical analysis. J Forens Sci. 1985, 30, 239-42.

1918. Zumwalt, R.E. & Hirsch, C.S. Subtle fatal child abuse. Hum Pathol. 1980, 11, 167-74.

1919. Zumwalt, R.E., Campbell, B., Balraj, E., Adelson, L. & Fransioli, M. Wounding characteristics of "shotshell" ammunition: a report of three cases. J Forens Sci. 1981, 1, 198-205.

INDEX

About the Compiler

ERNEST ABEL is a Professor at Wayne State University. He is the author of *A Dictionary of Drug Abuse Terms and Terminology* (Greenwood Press, 1984), and the compiler of *Behavioral Teratology: A Bibliography to the Study of Birth Defects of the Mind* (Greenwood Press, 1985), *Fetal Alcohol Exposure and Effects: A Comprehensive Bibliography* (Greenwood Press, 1985), *Narcotics and Reproduction: A Bibliography* (Greenwood Press, 1983), and numerous other works.

www.ingramcontent.com/pod-product-compliance
Lightning Source LLC
Chambersburg PA
CBHW050228270326
41914CB00003BA/617
* 9 7 8 0 3 1 3 2 5 9 0 1 2 *